ISBN 978-0-259-95745-4
PIBN 10832418

1 MONTH OF
FREE
READING

at

www.ForgottenBooks.com

By purchasing this book you are eligible for one month membership to ForgottenBooks.com, giving you unlimited access to our entire collection of over 1,000,000 titles via our web site and mobile apps.

To claim your free month visit: www.forgottenbooks.com/free832418

FIFTH ANNUAL REPORT

OF THE

;LASGOW EMANCIPATION SOCIETY:

HAVING FOR ITS OBJECTS

THE UNIVERSAL ABOLITION OF SLAVERY AND THE SLAVE TRADE;

HE PROTECTION OF THE RIGHTS OF THE ABORIGINAL INHABITANTS OF THE
BRITISH COLONIES;

AND THE BETTERING OF THE CONDITION OF OUR FELLOW-SUBJECTS,
THE NATIVES OF BRITISH INDIA.

ALSO,

REPORT OF THE LADIES' AUXILIARY SOCIETY.

Presented 1st August, 1839.

WITH AN APPENDIX,

)NTAINING SPEECHES AT THE ANNIVERSARY MEETING, LIST OF SUBSCRIBERS, ABSTRACT
OF THE CASH ACCOUNT OF BOTH SOCIETIES, AND MUCH IMPORTANT AND
INTERESTING INFORMATION.

GLASGOW:

PRINTED BY AIRD & RUSSELL, 75, ARGYLL STREET;
AND SOLD BY GEORGE GALLIE, BUCHANAN STREET;
J. SYMINGTON & CO., QUEEN STREET;
J. M'LEOD, ARGYLL STREET; D. ROBERTSON, TRONGATE;
AND WILLIAM SMEAL, GALLOWGATE.

ANNUAL MEETING.

ANNIVERSARY OF THE ABOLITION OF SLAVERY IN THE
BRITISH COLONIES.

GLASGOW, 1st *August*, 1839.

THIS Evening, the Fifth Annual Meeting of the *Glasgow Emancipation Society*, was held in George Street Chapel.

On the motion of Mr WILLIAM SMEAL, the Rev. Dr. WARDLAW, one of the Vice-Presidents of the Society, was called to the Chair.

The CHAIRMAN, having opened the business, and intimated that letters of apology, for absence, had been received from John Dennistoun, Esq., M.P.; the Rev. Professor Thomson and Dr. Burns, of Paisley; and from the Rev. William Johnston, of Limekilns; then called on Mr Murray, one of the Secretaries, to read an Abstract of the Annual Report; after which, Mr Smeal, the other Secretary, read the Report of the Committee of the *Ladies' Auxiliary*, and stated the amount received and disbursed by both Societies.   It was then—

I. Moved by the *Rev. Dr. Heugh*, and seconded by the *Rev. William Anderson* :—

" That the Reports now read by the Secretaries, be adopted as the Reports of the *Glasgow Emancipation Society*, and of the *Ladies' Auxiliary;* and that they be printed and circulated, under the direction of the respective Committees."

II. Moved by the *Rev. Archibald Baird*, of Paisley, and seconded by *John M'Leod, Esq.*, one of the Magistrates of Gorbals :—

" That the thanks of this Meeting are due to those Ministers and Congregations, who last year so cordially responded to the recommendation of this Society, both with respect to the observance of a time of Thanksgiving for the Abolition of Colonial Slavery, and the Collections in aid of our Funds; and this Meeting cherishes the hope, that these friends will continue to co-operate with us in the great Cause of Human Freedom."

III. Moved by the *Rev. Alexander Harvey*, and seconded by *John Maxwell, Esq., M.D.* :—

" That this Meeting rejoices in the formation of the London Society for promoting Universal Abolition; that we renew the expression of our fervent desire for the success of our Anti-Slavery brethren and sisters in America; and whilst, in common with the friends of Humanity everywhere, we deplore the continued existence and increased activity of the Traffic in Human Beings, we feel called upon to reiterate our conviction, that so long as Slavery is suffered to exist in any quarter of the Globe, the Slave Trade will never be effectually put down; and therefore resolve, under the Divine Blessing, to promote, to the utmost of our power, the Universal Extinction of Slavery."

IV. Moved by *Major-General Briggs*, and seconded by *William Craig, Esq.* :—

" That it is established by ample evidence, that there exists throughout British India—a country of vast extent and great fertility, whose inhabitants are intelligent and industrious, and whose ancient Institutions might be made instrumental to good government—an amount of destitution and misery, which demand the immediate sympathy and succour of the people of Great Britain."

V. Moved by *George Thompson, Esq.*, and seconded by *John S. Blyth, Esq.* :—

" That, considering the value of our Empire in India—the destitute and helpless condition of the many Millions of our Fellow-Subjects in that Country, and the intimate connexion between their Improvement and Prosperity as an Agricultural Population, and the Abolition of Slavery and the Slave Trade—this Meeting regards with the purest satisfaction the formation in London, of the BRITISH INDIA SOCIETY, and pledges itself to promote the great object which that Society has in view."

Dr. Wardlaw being obliged to leave the Meeting, was succeeded in the Chair by W. P. Paton, Esq.

The following Resolutions were carried by acclamation, viz. :—

VI. Moved by *George Thompson, Esq.* :—

" That the best thanks of this Meeting be given to Major-General Briggs, for the valuable and highly interesting information he has now communicated to this Society."

VII. Moved by *Thomas Grahame, Esq.* :—

" That the Offiee-Bearers and Committee of the Ladies' Auxiliary, and of this Society, be requested to continue their services :—
" That the cordial thanks of this Meeting be given to the Ladies, for their valuable co-operation :—and also,
" That the thanks of the Meeting be given to the Trustees, for the use of the Chapel ; and to Dr. Wardlaw for his conduct in the Chair."

RALPH WARDLAW, D.D., *Chairman.*

WILLIAM P. PATON, *Chairman.*

OFFICE-BEARERS.

President.

ROBERT GRAHAME, Esq., OF WHITEHILL.

Vice-Presidents.

REV. DR. WARDLAW, REV. DR. HEUGH, REV. DR. KIDSTON,
ANTHONY WIGHAM, Esq., Aberdeen.

Treasurer.

JAMES BEITH, Esq.,

Secretaries.

Messrs. JOHN MURRAY AND WILLIAM SMEAL.

Committee.

Rev. William Anderson.
William Auld.
William Brash.
John Duncan.
John Eadie.
John Edwards.
Greville Ewing.
Alexander Harvey.
John Johnstone.
David King.
William Lindsay.
J. M. M'Kenzie.
James M'Tear.
James Paterson.
Thomas Pullar.
Dr. Willis.
Messrs. David Anderson.
J. S. Blyth.
Hugh Brown.
William Brown.
Walter Buchanan.
Robert Connel.
William Craig.
G. C. Dick.

Messrs. William Ferguson.
John Fleming.
George Gallie.
Thomas Grahame.
Robert Kettle.
Henry Langlands.
Matthew Lethem.
Donald Macintyre.
John Maxwell, M.D.
Colin M'Dougal.
Ninian M'Gilp.
Anthony M'Keand.
David M'Laren.
John M'Leod.
William P. Paton.
John Reid.
Robert Sanderson.
James Stewart.
George Thorburn.
Archibald Watson.
George Watson.
James Watson.
William White.
Andrew Young.

Honorary and Corresponding Members.

GEORGE THOMPSON, Esq.
RIGHT HON. LORD BROUGHAM.
JOHN DENNISTOUN, Esq., M.P.
JOSEPH STURGE, Esq., Birmingham.
DANIEL O'CONNELL, Esq., M.P.
REV. THOMAS ROBERTS, Bristol.
REV. PATRICK BREWSTER, Paisley.
WILLIAM LLOYD GARRISON, Esq., Boston, New England.
ARTHUR TAPPAN, Esq., New York.
JAMES G. BIRNEY, Esq., do.
JAMES JOHNSTON, Esq., Upper Canada.
REV. NATHANIEL PAUL, Albany, New York.
JAMES M'CUNE SMITH, M.D., do.
M. GEORGE WASHINGTON LAFAYETTE, } Paris.
M. VICTOR DE TRACEY, }

REPORT.

Marking the progress of events in the Colonies, your Committee, at this time last year, drew upon them by anticipation. Thanksgivings were offered up to Him who overrules all things, and a Jubilee was held, in the confident expectation that Slavery, under the guise of Apprenticeship, had at last been abolished in the British West Indies.

It was even so—and now after a year of Freedom has revolved, we meet, not to mourn over desolate fields and deserted villages; not over a population rioting in anarchy and blood, as was predicted by the Enemies of Liberty, but to rejoice over a peaceable, an industrious, and a happy people.

Peaceable they are to an extreme; so that Militia and Police are deemed too superfluous to be worth the cost. On the subject of a Militia, the *Barbadoes Liberal* says,—" We tell Lord Normanby, plainly, openly, and boldly, that the Public of Barbadoes,—ninety-nine hundredths of the inhabitants of the Island, are perfectly satisfied that a Militia is not required." And, in reference to a Police Force, the *Jamaica Morning Journal* of June 3d observes,—" Not a single instance can be adduced of any necessity having arisen this year for such a body; and this being the case, the re-establishment of it must be regarded as a waste of the public funds.......In the mother country, nothing appears more essential than a police force. Here no one attaches the slightest importance to such a force, whilst its expence presents a serious objection to it. The peasantry are peaceable, quiet, and orderly—they may refuse to labour continuously, but certainly do not require policemen to keep them in order."

The Negroes are industrious, when their industry is rewarded by suitable compensation; but they will not work for those who give them not adequate wages for their labour; who over-reach them, and take advantage of them in every way in their power. No! They very properly mark them out, and take their labour to another market. There may not, on every estate, be the same number of labourers in the field; nor the same number of field labourers in the aggregate, as there was during Slavery; because some prefer other occupations—and the males, in general, seem disposed to permit the females to withdraw from the more laborious field operations, to domestic duties, while they themselves work harder, and thus make up in some measure for the deficiency of female labour. And there is not, upon the whole, so many invalids and delinquents withdrawn from field labour, as during the existence of Slavery.

Many estates, where the Negroes have been humanely treated, will yield, we are assured, their usual, or more than their usual, quantity of sugar; and whatever deficiency of crop may arise, will, we are confident, be more justly ascribed to the obstinacy, or something worse, of the Managers, than to the indolence of the Negroes. The Governor of Jamaica, while on a tour over the Island, told the Managers and Attorneys, in the presence of a large mixed assembly, that " white men were going about the country disguised as Policemen, pretending to have his authority, telling the people not to work." He said he "knew their intention and design—*he understood the trick.* You are anxious," said his Excellency, "to produce a panic, to reduce the value of property, to create dismay, in order that you may speculate by reducing the present value of property; but you will be disappointed, notwithstanding a press sends forth daily abuse against me, and blackguard and contemptible remarks against my acts. I assure you, *I am up to your tricks.*"

There has been a great deal of finesse among the Planters to make an appearance of a deficient crop—by keeping back shipments, expecting a rise of price, and by other stratagems. There will, doubtless, be a deficiency on some estates, owing to disagreements between the Managers and the Negroes; but all these matters, like the scum on a fermenting vessel, will, in due time, pass off, and all will soon settle down clear and pure. These trifling matters, with a little care and attention, will speedily remedy themselves. There is not a superabundance of labourers, and those who wish their estates to be cultivated, will have to change their obstinate and contentious Managers, and to pay a fair value for labour.

There is a stronger desire to import labourers than to treat with kindness, humanity, and justice, those already imported;

for whether they are Portuguese, Germans, or Hill Coolies, they soon find their way—to the grave. The Court of Policy of Guiana has voted to raise a loan of £400,000 for the immigration scheme. The Gladstone Slave Trade—not less the disgrace of the Government who permitted it, than of the man who, for his own avaricious purposes, prevailed upon them to institute the iniquitous traffic—has been the means of transporting from Calcutta, 5,886 Hill Coolies; 5,379 to the Mauritius, and 414 to Guiana—settlements equally famed for cruelty. Of these latter, the *Guiana Royal Gazette* asks, "where are the Portuguese that were imported here? and where will the Hill Coolies soon be? Of the seventy or eighty located on Belle Vue estate (Mr Gladstone's) about a year ago, it appears that *not more than fifteen or sixteen are fit to go to the field* at the present time." And on an examination into their treatment on that estate before W. B. Woolsely, Esq., Assistant Government Secretary, and a Magistrate, Mr W. said, " I never saw such a dreadful scene of misery in my life, as is now to be seen in the sick house. I have been in a great many hospitals on various estates for the last twenty years, but *I never saw so melancholy a scene !*" Mr Matthews, the attorney for the estate, replied—" Oh, they are *acclimatizing*, that is all I can say about it !"

In answer to questions put to Mr Labouchere on this subject, in the House of Commons, on the 24th July, he said that " the condition of the Hill Coolies of Demerara had been one generally of disease and mortality; and abundant proof had reached the Colonial Office, that too much vigilance could not be exercised to prevent the cruelties and hardships to which they were subjected by strangers." (*Times*, July 25.) On the 27th we find another version, by way of correction, of what he had previously stated. " He had stated that the general condition of the Hill Coolies in Demerara was not [?] one of general disease or mortality, although there was abundant proof of their being exposed to hardships which called for considerable vigilance on the part of Government. He had since looked more accurately into the returns of mortality, and he was bound to take the earliest opportunity of correcting that statement, by mentioning to the House, that though the mortality was not so great in any part of the Island* as on the particular estate of which mention had been made, yet the total mortality throughout the Island did not show that the general

* The Geography of the Hon. Gentleman, or of his Reporter, is at fault here, in speaking of Demerara as an *Island*.

condition was one of health. There was not a particle of information which the Colonial Office possessed on this subject which would not be printed and laid before the House in the course of a few days."

It is some consolation, however, to know from the same authority, " that the order against further importation of Coolies has been strictly enforced;"—and that at last, " on 31st March, the final and complete Emancipation of the Apprenticed labourers in the Mauritius had taken place, in a peaceable and satisfactory manner."

In Antigua, where they wisely preferred *Immediate* Emancipation to Apprenticeship, and have had five years of freedom, the Rev. Mr Gilbert, an extensive proprietor and resident in the island, says,—" If due allowance is made for the drought of 1837, I have little doubt that the crops of the first five years of freedom, will equal, or nearly so, the last five years of Slavery. Estates that had not been cultivated in the memory of man, are once more crowned with cane fields, and I have myself re-established a set of works which had been in a state of dilapidation for more than twenty years."

Our excellent Anti-Slavery friends, Charles Stuart, and John Scoble, Esqs., have gone out to the West Indies, and are investigating the working of the system, and exposing its defects; and Dr. Palmer, formerly a Special Magistrate, and late editor of the *British Emancipator*, has resumed his residence in Jamaica, where he has established a Newspaper, entitled, *The Colonial Reformer:* so that the interests of the Emancipated classes will be closely watched. What a pity that this is necessary.

Schools and Churches are being built in great numbers, and education is ardently sought after by the Emancipated Negroes. A proposal has been made in Jamaica, to send out a Mission from the West Indies to Africa, under the charge of the Rev. William Knibb, and an institution is to be established in Jamaica for the training of Negro Missionaries. We are informed, indeed, by a letter from Mr Knibb, to Dr. Hoby of Birmingham, that " one of the despised and traduced sons of Africa has left Jamaica, taking with him only a letter of recommendation from his late pastor, Mr Gardner,—has worked his passage to Africa, and, without any support or countenance, except from God, is now on the spot from whence he was stolen when a boy, *telling his countrymen of the name of Jesus ;* and although he does not know Greek or Latin, he knows and feels that Jesus died to save sinners, and in the spirit of an apostle he has gone to proclaim his precious name. A pious medical gentleman in one of the Queen's ships, just from Africa, saw Thomas Keith, (that is his name,) there, and he appears to enter very warmly into his subject. Several other interesting blacks are ready to go,"—and are probably away before now.

The Negroes in Canada, many of them refugees from United States' Slavery, are forming, with the co-operation of the Whites, Anti-Slavery Societies, to promote the liberation of the Slaves of the Republic.

Altogether, the result of British Colonial Emancipation is truly gratifying, whether we regard it on the Continent of America or of Africa,—at Guiana or the Cape,—on islands, large or small,—from St. Lucia, with its 2,000, to Jamaica with its 300,000 persons liberated at once—and where the numbers greatly exceeded those of the resident whites—liberated too, in spite of the obstructions thrown in the way by interested Planters—by men addicted to oppression, almost constitutionally attached to Slavery, whose characters seem as unchangeable as the leopard's spots, or the Ethiopian's skin, unless operated upon through the opening of their eyes to see, that by the boon of Freedom to the Slave, their own aggrandizement will be promoted. The result of Emancipation, we repeat, is truly gratifying, and well calculated to exercise a beneficial effect on the Abolition of the Slave System elsewhere; especially in the United States, where the subject is often referred to, both in Anti-Slavery and other publications. Thus we are encouraged still to persevere in promoting, by every means in our power, the Abolition of Slavery throughout the world, as the sure means of extinguishing the Slave Trade.

The Emancipation infection has begun to spread to the Foreign Islands in the Carribean Archipelago. Cuba has taken the alarm, and has issued a decree, prohibiting intercourse with the Emancipated. But decrees will not prevent men from longing for, and finally obtaining liberty.

It appears that two respectable American gentlemen were ordered off the Island, because they were suspected to be Abolitionists. And the Agent of the *British and Foreign Bible Society* says, that the Archbishop of Cuba had issued a circular, in which the people were warned of the attempt that would be made to circulate the Bible, and thereby to stir up the Slaves to assassinate their masters! At Santiago de Cuba, although furnished with most respectable letters of introduction, he again fell under suspicion of being a person sent to disturb the public peace and order of the Island. He was put upon oath by the authorities of the city, and subjected to a severe and lengthened examination, as to his objects, designs, and movements, and then directed to leave without delay. A case of Bibles, consigned to him from Kingston, was seized and detained, (perhaps suspecting them to be *Anti-Slavery* publications—*as in truth they were*,) and he himself escaped with some difficulty from the Island,—an order for his arrest and imprisonment arriving, as it would seem, the day after he embarked.

Strange opinions are produced in Governments, according to the degree of liberty enjoyed. While Jamaica had Slaves, she was very jealous of holding any intercourse with the Free Black Republicans of Hayti; but now the tables are turned, and Hayti is jealous of intercourse with Jamaica, because the principles of liberty and of Government are too freely discussed in that Island to suit the Haytian taste as an article of import. But here, too, liberal principles will work their way.

Hitherto we have been giving a Report, rather of the result of our Abolition efforts on the Emancipated, than of our operations for the past year ; yet it surely cannot be inappropriate, briefly to trace, how far this branch of the object of your Society has been accomplished.

The absolute safety, as well as the advantages of Immediate and Entire Emancipation, have been most satisfactorily demonstrated ; if the safety and advantages of obeying the command of God, of doing justice and loving mercy, could ever be questioned by men professing to be Christians. But after all, compared with the vast field before us, all that has yet been accomplished may be regarded only as an experiment, just as the skilful artizan or chemist operates on a small scale, to put any new or great principle to the test.

France has declared free, after remaining seven years in the service of Government, all Negroes, whose names are not inscribed on any district register, or to whom no Planter can produce an incontrovertible claim, although such Negroes may be unable to prove their freedom. The National Institute has proposed the question of the Abolition of Slavery for a Prize Essay.

The enterprising Pasha of Egypt, Mehemet Ali, has set an example to Christian Governments worthy of their imitation. He makes it his study to promote the education, interests, and happiness of his people. Although a follower of the Maho-

medan religion, which justifies the enslavement of infidels, he
has strictly prohibited the Gazou, or Slave-hunt, by which his
army was supplied, and his officers appropriated to themselves
captured Slaves for the arrears of their pay;—ordered that
quarrels between neighbouring tribes be adjusted by the
Governor-General;—set the example of paying wages to his
people;—abolished Slavery among the Negro tribes, which
was the source of constant wars, and has encouraged them
to cultivate the soil.

Our American Anti-Slavery brethren congratulate the
friends of free institutions, that the doctrine of *Immediate
Emancipation* is now established on a basis from which it
cannot be dislodged, either by the malice of its enemies, or
the unfaithfulness of its friends.

Three hundred and four new Societies have been added last
year, making the total 1,650, and their funds are also increased.

The press is more extensively discussing or advocating the
freedom of the Slave.

The American Anti-Slavery Society has issued 724,862
publications during the year.

·In the Southern States, it may be said the whites as well as
the blacks are enslaved; but, that a change is proceeding,
there is evidence which cannot at present be produced, without
endangering the lives of parties in that quarter.

The agitation and discussion of the subject in the Churches,
is producing strange work. The General Assembly of the
Presbyterian Church is rent asunder, and divided into two
jealous and hostile sects.

In the Methodist Episcopal Church, sentiments equally op-
posite and incongruous are held, while the Anti-Slavery Society looks quietly on, and is steadily progressing, gratified
that these champions of Slavery, headed by a bishop, who
quotes the golden rule as good authority for Slave-holding,
have, by their contests, advanced the cause of Abolition.

In Congress, the right of petition has been the fourth time
refused; nevertheless, under all these discouragements, these
noble-hearted Abolitionists persevere. Let us cheer them on,
by extending to them the right hand of fellowship. *They*
cordially wish us God speed in our endeavours to improve the
condition of our *Eastern* fellow-subjects, and we may well
reciprocate the feeling on their behalf.

The onward march of the cause in the United States, is most
graphically described in the following extract of a letter addressed to Wendell Phillips, Esq., (an eminent Abolitionist now

in this country,) by the Board of Managers of the Massachusetts Anti-Slavery Society :—

" In the year 1829, an isolated drop appeared on the surface of the land; in the year 1839, that drop is swallowed up and lost in a great ocean of humanity, which is swelling and dashing against the walls of the American Bastile with a might that is irresistible.   Ten years ago, a solitary indivi. dual stood up as the advocate of Immediate and Unconditional Emancipa. tion, with scarcely one to cheer him to the conflict with American slavery. Now that individual sees around him, in amicable league, hundreds of thousands of persons, of both sexes, members of every sect and party, from the most elevated to the humblest rank in life, the rich and the poor, the learned and the ignorant.   In 1829, not an Anti-Slavery Society, of a genuine stamp, was in existence.   In 1839, there are nearly two thousand societies, swarming and multiplying in all parts of the free States.   In 1829, there was but one Anti-Slavery periodical in the land.   Now there are not less than fourteen.   In 1829, scarcely a newspaper, of any reli- gious sect or political party, was willing to disturb the ' delicate ' question of Slavery.   In 1839, there are multitudes of journals that either openly advocate the doctrine of Immediate Emancipation, or permit its free dis- cussion in their columns.   In 1829, scarcely one tract or pamphlet, in opposition to American slavery, could be readily found.   In 1839, it is impossible to calculate the whole number that is scattered over the land, thicker than rain-drops, and as nourishing to the soil of freedom.   Includ- ing the issues of the regular Anti-Slavery periodicals, the estimate may be safely reckoned by millions.   In 1829, not an Anti-Slavery agent was in the field; now there are scores, whose labours are as untiring as their appeals prove irresistible.   In 1829, a Lecture on Slavery was an anomaly.   In 1839, the Lectures and Sermons delivered on this subject are too numerous to be estimated.   Ten years ago, scarcely an ecclesiastical or political body dared to assail, even indirectly, the Slave system.   Now, synods, confer- ences, general associations, and legislative assemblies, are lifting up their voices against its continuance.   Then, hardly a church, of any denomina- tion, made slaveholding a bar to communion and Christian fellowship ; now, multitudes refuse to hear a slaveholder preach, or to recognize him as a brother.   In 1829, scarcely one, if any petition, was sent to Congress, praying for the Abolition of Slavery in the District of Columbia, &c., &c. Now, in one day, a single member of the House of Representatives, (John Quincy Adams,) has presented one hundred and seventy-six in de- tail.   It was ascertained, at the last session but one, that not less than seven hundred thousand persons had memorialized Congress on this and kindred subjects.   In 1829, that scourge of the coloured race, and most in- human association, the American Colonization Society, was flourishing like a green bay-tree, having secured the approbation of both Church and State, and laughing to scorn all opposition.   In 1839, there are few so poor as to do it reverence, in the free States,—though the traffickers ' in Slaves and the souls of men ' regard it as the sheet anchor of their piratical ship.   Its popularity has given place to abhorrence—its honour is changed to infamy—and it lies prostrate, helpless, bankrupt—a broken and blasted monument of God's displeasure.   In 1829, where ten Slaves escaped from their prison-house, now a hundred find their way to the north, and are safely landed in Canada, to receive liberty and protection under the flag of Vic- toria.   May their numbers increase, from day to day, and from hour to hour, and God send them a good deliverance, is the prayer of every true- hearted abolitionist.   In 1829, the Free Coloured Population of the United

States were bowed to the earth in despair. Before the combined influences of those twin-monsters, Slavery and Colonization, they withered like a green herb in a time of drought. Their spirits were broken, their energies paralyzed, their expectations of future good cut off. In 1839, they are quickened into life (through the power of Abolitionism) as by a mighty resurrection. Now they begin to be filled with the spirit of enterprise, and are eager for moral and intellectual improvement. In various places, they have well-furnished libraries, debating societies, scientific clubs, temperance and moral reform societies, &c., &c. They have also two periodicals, very ably conducted, by men of their own complexion. Two of their members are members of the executive Committee of the American Anti-Slavery Society, and are thus practically entrusted with the management of the Anti-Slavery enterprise. But we must forbear. The contrast between the state of things in 1829 and at the present time, (which we have barely glanced at,) presents almost miraculous transformations to the vision of every candid person. No revolution in public sentiment, during the same time, has ever been more extraordinary, more hopeful, or more important. Truly, before heaven and earth we attest, that it is solely the Lord's doing, and it is very marvellous in all eyes. Shall not He, then, have all the glory.

" Tell our British brethren, that the apathy which once brooded over the land, like a spell of death, is broken for ever. Tell them there is no part of our immense national domain, which is not agitated with the great question of human rights. For into what circle or society, what political or religious body, what legislative or ecclesiastical assembly, has the discussion not been carried? What a mass of intellect has been quickened, what generous sympathy for the oppressed excited, what intense abhorrence of Slavery every where called into activity! Yea, what sacrifices have been made, what labours and sufferings joyfully encountered, by multitudes, that the yokes and fetters of twenty-five hundred thousand American bondmen might be broken, at once and for ever! We do not believe, that what brought the people of England to repentance, in America serves to harden the national heart;—that the same principles, which, on moral and religious grounds, effected the Abolition of Slavery in one country, are calculated to perpetuate that horrid system, by their promulgation in another.

" Among the distinguished band of British philanthropists, whom it will be your privilege to take by the hand, will doubtless be our beloved and eloquent coadjutor, GEORGE THOMPSON. Joyful, most joyful, will be the meeting between you. Convey to him the renewed assurances of our gratitude for his invaluable services in this country, our admiration of his philanthropic labours in Great Britain, and our deep interest in his present and future welfare. There are thousands and thousands in this country, who are fondly anticipating the time when he will again visit the United States. In his new field of benevolent enterprise, we heartily bid him God speed, as well as all those who are associated with him."

Very soon after the period of last Annual Meeting, that devoted friend of oppressed humanity, Mr George Thompson, having become connected with the *British and Foreign Aborigines Protection Society*, as their Agent, visited Glasgow along with Mr. Montgomery Martin, a Member of their Committee. These gentlemen met your Committee on the 6th of September last, when they were heard in explanation of the objects and prospects of that Association; and after the Committee had deliberated on the matter, particularly in reference to the condition of many Millions of our fellow-subjects in British India; and the Members present had expressed their sentiments thereon,—it was moved, seconded, and unanimously resolved, that a junction with the *Aborigines Society* should take place, and that the designation of your Society should be altered to embrace the purposes of both; which resolution, at a Public Meeting held the same evening, was fully confirmed.

In commending the very important object which the Society for the Protection of the Aborigines has in view, and the claim which it therefore has on our assistance and co-operation, we cannot do better than refer to an Appeal which it has lately published in London:—

"This Society, which was instituted in 1836, advocates the cause of many millions of human beings, a large portion of them intimately connected with British Colonies and commerce. They are the free Aborigines of remote countries, whom experience proves, when justly and kindly treated, to be capable of receiving the benefits of Civilization and Christianity, while they urgently require protection in their increasing conflicts against oppression.

"Of these people, the Aborigines who may be termed British, amount, at a low estimate, to one million inhabiting Australia; one million in the South Sea Islands, including New Zealand; half a million still surviving in North and South America; and two millions in Western and Southern Africa, with several millions of the more barbarous tribes in British India and its borders, and of the Eastern Archipelago and Indian Ocean.

"Of Foreign Aborigines, who will be benefited by our efforts, there are sixteen millions in America; sixty millions in Africa; two hundred millions in Asia; and a small but interesting remnant of ancient European barbarism existing in Lapland.

"Among these multitudinous tribes our imported diseases produce frightful ravages; our ardent spirits deprave and consume their population; our unjust laws exclude them from enjoying that first element of well-ordered societies—judicial protection, as well as from the possibility of a timely incorporation with Colonial communities; while, in addition to all these evils, our neglect of suitable methods of improving them, prevents their adopting the civilized manners and customs to which they are inclined.

"The Aborigines Protection Society seeks to devise remedies for these evils, and its plan of operation embraces,

"1st. An extensive correspondence at home and abroad.

"2d. The publication of documents and papers.

"3d. Interviews and communications with different departments of the State.

"4th. The presentation of petitions to the Crown and to the Legislature.

"The extension of Colonies constitutes a marked characteristic of the times we live in, to which fertile source of national prosperity, the course pursued by the Aborigines Protection Society is by no means opposed. But it is impossible for us as men, patriots, philanthropists, or Christians, to behold without anxiety the ruin of the people we shall be thus accessary in supplanting, unless our future modes of colonization be directed with greater humanity and wisdom than in times past.

" The claim of this society to public support is rested on the grounds already briefly stated, and as its funds arise from voluntary contributions, the Committee earnestly solicit annual subscriptions or donations."

It is obviously quite competent for your Society to co-operate with this Institution in its benevolent plans ; and, at the same time, to pursue with unabated zeal our original object, which at the formation of the Society in 1833 was declared to be—*The Abolition of Slavery throughout the World.* The language of the 2d Resolution passed at our first Annual Meeting, contains a further expression of the *Glasgow Emancipation Society's* object. " Contemplating the appalling statement made in the Report, that there are *Five Millions* of the human race in a state of the most abject Slavery, and the dreadful extent to which it appears the Slave Trade is still carried on—of all the horrors and atrocities of which traffic, *Slavery is the fruitful source,*—Resolve to continue, and if possible increase their exertions, for the *removal of the one* and the *annihilation of the other.*"

Such was the ground which your Society took up, immediately after the Imperial Abolition Act was passed ; but having lately had its efforts directed principally to the Extinction of our Colonial Slavery, under the name of Apprenticeship ; and having now satisfactory proof of its entire termination, in a way likely to have considerable influence upon Foreign Slavery and the Slave Trade, your Committee trust their constituents are ready to direct all their energies to that very important subject, and that the inhabitants of Glasgow, *regarding all mankind as their brethren,* will extend to *them* the same zealous sympathy which they manifested for their fellow-subjects, by their numerously signed petitions in their behalf.

Order of time seems to require, that your Committee should notice here the severe loss they have sustained, by the death of two of their number, since our last Annual Meeting. We mean, John M'Leod, and Patrick Lethem, Esqs. These Gentlemen were among the earliest and warmest friends of the Slave.— Hence, their absence is deeply felt by your Committee, as a deprivation to the cause they so earnestly seek to promote. And regret for the decease of these truly humane, benevolent, and Christian individuals, is not confined to the members of

c

this Society, but is universally felt by all those institutions, which aim to promote the temporal or spiritual interests of our fellow-men. Mr M'Leod, it will be recollected, perished along with his estimable friend, Mr James Perston, in the melancholy wreck of the Forfarshire Steam-packet; and your Committee participate in the sympathy which has been so generally expressed for their families, under the peculiarly afflicting dispensation which was permitted to befal them.

Mr Lethem's liberality, as a contributor to the funds of this Society, and his unflinching zeal in the great cause of Universal Abolition, will ever entitle his memory to the cordial esteem of your Committee; and it is their fervent prayer to God,— "all whose works are truth, and his ways judgment,"—that the mantles of those whom He has seen fit to remove, may fall upon suitable successors.

There having appeared, in the Life of the late Mr Wilberforce, published by his sons, certain statements prejudicial to the hitherto undisputed claim of the venerable Thomas Clarkson, Esq., to be regarded as the primary promoter and advocate of the Abolition of the Slave Trade; your Committee deemed it right to express, by a special Resolution on the subject, their estimation of Mr Clarkson's labours, as the chief instrument, under Providence, of accomplishing not only the termination of the heinous traffic in Slaves, but also of the system of Slavery which existed in the British Colonies. The following Resolution, prepared by your Committee, was unanimously approved by a public meeting of their fellow-citizens, at the close of one of Mr Thompson's Lectures, on the 14th November last, and a copy was transmitted to Mr Clarkson :—

"The Glasgow Emancipation and Aborigines' Protection Society— lately the Glasgow Emancipation Society—in Public Meeting assembled, considering that their labours in the latter character are almost entirely brought to a favourable termination as regards the British Colonies, by the complete enfranchisement of the Slaves there on the 1st of August last, followed by the most cheering and satisfactory accounts of the orderly and decorous manner in which they received their new-born liberty, and have since conducted themselves: In consideration also of the successful issue of the cause, and of the advanced age of THOMAS CLARKSON, Esq., now in his 78th year, who has steadily and perseveringly devoted 53 years of his life to its promotion—Resolve, That this Society feel themselves, on the present occasion, particularly called upon to declare, that, duly appreciating the very important services of Mr Wilberforce in Parliament, which perhaps none other there could have rendered to the same extent, yet they believe that he was much indebted for his materials to MR CLARKSON, who, in point of priority, preceded Mr Wilberforce in drawing public attention to the subject of the Slave Trade and Slavery ; and that to MR CLARKSON, *more than to any other individual,* out of Parliament, has the cause been indebted, for long and well-directed, diligent, persevering, un-tiring, unostentatious, and self-devoted effort—and, in particular, it was by his labours in 1822, by making a tour through the kingdom, and arousing the slumbering Anti-Slavery spirit; in resuscitating and establishing So-cieties for the abolition of Slavery; and by his publications on the subject, that the people were then stimulated to seek from the Legislature the Emancipation of the Slave; and since, encouraged by a variety of circum-stances, and the co-operation of many influential individuals, have perse-vered, until they have obtained its final accomplishment.

"That this Society, therefore, publicly tender to THOMAS CLARKSON, Esq., their hearty congratulations on the peaceful and happy results of his, their, and the country's exertions in the Anti-Slavery cause, and on the prospects likely to accrue therefrom to the liberty of the human race throughout the world; and they hope that, by the blessing of God, he may yet be long spared to witness and enjoy, in the decline of life, these cheering fruits of his early and uninterrupted labours.

"RALPH WARDLAW, D.D., *Chairman.*"

In reference to this matter, the same course was simultan-eously adopted by many other Anti-Slavery Associations in the kingdom; and the Common Council of the City of Lon-don decreed, that a marble bust of Mr Clarkson should imme-diately be erected, as a testimony to future generations, of his humane and praiseworthy efforts to promote the happiness of his fellow-creatures.

Allusion has already been made to Five Millions still in Slavery —but this, although a vast number,—equal to twenty times the population of Glasgow—is far below the mark. This was the amount estimated several years ago, as held by Christian nations!—nations nominally Christian. Of these, two millions two hundred and fifty thousand were held by the United States of America; but with their increase, and the addition of those in Texas—which from their friendship for it may be regarded as part of the territory of the United States*—three millions may therefore now be put down under that head;† and with those held in Slavery by Mahomedans, and in India, altogether they may, at the present time, perhaps be more correctly esti-mated at Eight Millions. Thus, only a *tithe* of this number are yet freed!!

In a work which Mr Buxton has lately published, on the Afri-can Slave Trade, and which we strongly recommend to all who take an interest in this direful subject, the number of human be-

---

* For further information on the subject of Texas, and its anticipated incor-poration with the United States, see Appendix, No. II.

† Whether for good or ill we know not; but it appears that the Slaves in the United States are not to be distinguished as such in their future census. If from a sense of shame, this may be for good; if merely to conceal their evil deeds from the world's eye, little benefit may be expected from the step.

ings carried into Slavery, or murdered in the process, is estimated, on a very moderate calculation, and from well authen-
ticated testimony, to be as follows :—

Annually subjected to the horrors of Slavery,		120,000
Murdered in the seasoning,	30,000	
Murdered in the middle passage,	37,000	
Murdered in the march, seizure, and detention,	187,000	255,000
Annual victims of the Christian Slave Trade,		375,000
Annual victims of the Mohamedan Trade,		100,000
Annual loss to Africa,		475,000

Or more than a thousand per day sacrificed to the demon of
Slavery, by nations calling themselves Christian ! ! !

Let us, if we can, contemplate the magnitude of this object.
Let us, as men and as Christians, endeavour to grasp in our
imaginations, the vast extent of moral, civil, political, and physical evil connected with the holding in Slavery of Eight Millions
of our fellow-creatures, and the feeding of the insatiable maw
of this monster with *a thousand human victims every day.* Let
us reflect upon the immense amount of wretchedness and cruelty involved in this system—the tearing asunder of the kindred
ties of nature and affection—the pains, the groans, and the cruel
deaths—not only the sufferings of the enslaved, but the sin of
the enslavers, and its awful and eternal consequences ; and can
we then unconcernedly fold our arms in indolence, and be in-
sensible to the call of duty. We trust not—but that the magnitude of the object will be a stimulus to our exertions.

But it may be asked, by what means is this object to be
accomplished ? Here your Committee would revert to some
remarks on this subject, and some measures in reference to
it, which were proposed in their First Report:—

"It must be remembered, that it is now with foreign powers holding
Slaves, that our business lies ; and that the measures to be pursued in each
particular case, must be carefully and judiciously considered ; must be
adapted to the peculiar circumstances of each ; and be prudently and
cautiously prosecuted. The jealousy of foreign interference, so natural
to every state, precludes us from resorting to such measures with foreign
Slave-holding powers, as we brought to bear on our own Government.
We have no reason to expect, that a direct appeal from us to these Governments would be listened to. Hence, the only course left open for us,
is to use every means we can, to induce the subjects of foreign states to
consider, with the attention which it demands, the question of the Emanci-
patiou of their fellow-subjects from Slavery ; and, if we succeed in im-
pressing a portion of them, influential from circumstances or number, with
its importance, we must leave it to them to urge their respective Governments to carry that Emancipation into effect. It may also materially tend
to promote the cause, if we can, at the same time, induce our Government

to use its influence on this subject, in its negotiations with foreign powers. But our success in this, must very much depend upon the *character* of the Government. It would be in vain to propose such a measure to those at present in power.* The Committee trust, however, that this obstacle to the progress of Liberty and Liberal measures, will soon be removed out of the way ; never more to interfere with the affairs of this kingdom, or to retard the progress of Liberty in foreign states.

" And here, in passing, the Committee cannot omit the opportunity of reminding the friends of liberal measures—the advocates for a liberal Government, who have lately so nobly distinguished themselves, and shown by how much they outnumber their opponents, how closely *their* cause and *ours* is allied ; and of expressing to them our regret, that a greater proportion of them have not joined our standard. *We,*—to a man, will be found in *their* ranks ; why then, may not *they* join *us ?*— *They* seek to advance their own, and their Nation's liberty ; and without using any direct means to accomplish it, leave that of others to follow, as it may in process of time, as a matter of course. But whilst *in common with them,* we unite in the means used to advance our National liberty, we would not leave to their fate, our most destitute fellow-men in other countries, who are suffering all the miseries, and degradation, and cruelty of Slavery, even under professedly liberal Governments, without the power to help themselves,—but would ' remember them that are in bonds,' and use every effort in our power, to ' let the oppressed' in *every land* ' go free.' As the friends of liberal measures, then, love Liberty for themselves, we would earnestly call upon them to endeavour to impart it to others—to give to *this* Society, and its *object,* all the weight of their influence ;—for they may be assured, that while there are Five Millions of their fellow-men in Slavery throughout the world, and of these, Two and a half Millions under one of the reputedly freest Governments on the earth, genuine liberty cannot flourish. Slavery, and Slave-holding Governments, be they Regal, or Republican, are the natural soil of oppression and despotism ; and we would warn our Trans-Atlantic brethren, that no Government, call it Republican or by what name they may, can long continue to flourish, and to dispense, *even to the free,* the unadulterated blessings of Liberty, if it cherish Slavery within its dominion—if *more than one-sixth of its subjects are Slaves ;* they cherish in their bosom a reptile that will one day sting them to the core. On the other hand, we may anticipate, that the happy circumstance of the extinction of Slavery in the British Colonies, and, we may add, of Slave-holders from the Councils of this nation, will, in a thousand ways unperceived, shed its benign influence over the advancement of our National freedom.

" In prosecution of the general object of your Society, one of your Secretaries forwarded to Lord Suffield, and to Mr Buxton, copies of an Address to His Majesty, praying that he would be graciously pleased to order Returns to be made, and information to be obtained and laid before Parliament, by the various authorities residing at Sierra Leone, or at the Courts of Foreign Slave-holding powers, and by the Officers of Vessels of War, relative to such cases of Slave-Trading, as may have occurred during the last five years, or since the last papers on this subject were laid before Parliament, that it might be seen to what extent the Slave Trade has been carried on, notwithstanding the Treaties with Foreign powers, and the laws made for its prohibition. And that, seeing thereby the ineffi-

* This was during the Peel and Wellington administration.

ciency of all the means used for its suppression, and considering that the only effectual method of accomplishing its entire extinction, is the Total and Universal Abolition of Slavery, that His Majesty would be graciously pleased to instruct his Minister for Foreign affairs, and the authorities re. siding at the Courts of Foreign States, to enter into a friendly correspon. dence with these Governments, so as prevail upon them to Emancipate their bondsmen.

" This address was sent to Lord Suffield and Mr Buxton, not with the intention of immediate presentation, but rather to consult them as to this mode of forwarding our object—or whether, instead of the several Societies sending such addresses to His Majesty, it would not be preferable, to endeavour, through their respective Members, to get addresses presented from both Houses of Parliament.

" Letters were received, in reply, from Mr Buxton, and Lord Suffield, dated 24th and 25th February, 1834. Lord Suffield, whilst he recommended Addresses through Parliament, as preferable—and expressed his desire in common with us, to see Slavery abolished throughout the world ; yet from the jealousy that exists in America of all interference from this country, he did not advise the measures we proposed, immediately. Mr Buxton stated, that he concurred with us in thinking our work but very partially done, until we have seen the Emancipation of all Slaves in all countries ; and that he would confer with the friends of the cause, on the suggestion of an Address by Parliament to the King.

" These gentlemen, so eminently distinguished by their zeal for the extinction of British Colonial Slavery, although they expressed themselves confident that the Abolition scheme would work well—were yet desirous to delay the prosecution of the measures which our Society contemplated, till we might have it in our power to refer to ' Prosperity, the result of peace, good order, and industry established in our Colonies'—and to ' Experience, for a proof of the advantages, commercial, moral and religious, resulting from Emancipation.'

" Your Committee, although not entirely agreeing with these opinions, did not, however, press the measure further at that time, rather reserving it till they should see, which they hope will soon be the case, these enlightened philanthropists in the ranks of those devoted to the cause of Universal Abolition, and taking a lead in the British and Foreign Society,* for promoting that most desirable object."

A change of Ministry took place shortly after the period to which your Committee have referred, and they have now been several years in office. But the complexion of their policy on this question has been of so doubtful a character, that we fear, if we are to judge from their opposition to the Abolition of the Apprenticeship, and their sanctioning so readily the Hill Coolie Slave Trade, their sensitiveness on the subject is not of the very quickest kind. They will not, your Committee believe, be self-inclined to adopt any very effective measures in this cause, unless forced upon them by the pressure from without, or by the altered circumstances of our Colonies. There is

* The Society then existing under that name in London has, we believe, died a natural death; and the one formed there on 18th April last, with a similar name, is a different society.

little to be expected from their moral perceptions on the matter, and hence it will, in all probability, be necessary to resort to Addresses or Memorials to them and the Crown, through Parliament, as we formerly proposed. However, now that every remnant of Slavery is happily extinct in all our Colonies, we may cherish a hope that the Ministry and the Colonial proprietors at home will, ere long, become warm advocates for the Abolition of Slavery and the Slave Trade in other quarters. The people of Jamaica have already been appealing to the Government on the subject.

Your Committee trust, that the Anti-Slavery public of the United Kingdom, who have so long and so steadily struggled in the contest, will not think of retiring from the field because victory has crowned their efforts with success in one small department, while ten times the number rescued still remain exposed to the tender mercies of the Slave-holder; and Africa, whose only crime is, that she is offenseless and defenceless, is regarded as a reserve to supply the waste of human life, occasioned by the cruelty and the drudgery required to minister to the wants and luxuries of her more polished barbarian neighbours; but that, stimulated by success, Abolitionists will stretch their views to more extensive fields of enterprise. Whilst each individual and each society should act as faithfully, and as energetically, as if the work depended on their separate exertions, it is encouraging to know, that there are several Anti-Slavery Associations throughout the Kingdom engaged in the same contest; and many more, it is to be hoped, will be found to co-operate in the work. Your Committee are disposed to regard it as an earnest of continued and successful exertion in this great cause, that a Meeting, to which we were invited to send Delegates, was held in London on the 18th of April last, which issued in the formation of " The British and Foreign Anti-Slavery Society," for the Abolition of Slavery and the Slave Trade throughout the world. Mr George Thompson and the Rev. Dr. Wardlaw were appointed to represent the Glasgow Emancipation Society; but while we hailed with pleasure the formation of this kindred Institution in the metropolis, we proposed to co-operate, not as an Auxiliary, but as an independent Society.

The Slave Trade is indeed prosecuted at present with great activity, as if the parties were apprehensive that their harvest of human victims was soon to be ended. " The children of this world are in their generation wiser than the children of light." Let *their* activity stimulate us to use every justifiable means for the advancement of our cause, and as that cause is one of justice and mercy, we may reasonably expect to succeed. A project has simultaneously originated in America, England, and Scotland, to hold a Conference of Anti-Slavery Delegates from all parts of the world, in London, in the summer of 1840, and the London British and Foreign Anti-Slavery Society have proposed that it should commence on the 12th June next. We trust much good will result from this measure; and that it will be the means of diffusing a more extended and right principled feeling of sympathy for the sufferings of the Slave and of Africa, which may sow the seeds of future effort in their behalf, in the respective countries from which the Delegates may come.

Let us never despair while we have the moral energy and influence of the British nation on our side, and on the side of the oppressed; and this we trust we shall now have with us more than ever. Great Britain now stands out on a high moral eminence, which cannot fail to induce respect and attention to every thing she may say or do on this interesting question. And if the interference of Great Britain, France, and Russia, to protect 810,000 Greeks from the oppression of the Turks in 1827, was justifiable and commendable; how much more so—nay, would it not be a high moral duty in Great Britain—to throw the shield of her protection over the hundred millions of Africa—degraded and outcast Africa pillaged of her inhabitants—and now that the hands of Britain are clean from any participation in Slavery or the Slave Trade, she is in a fit state to say to all other powers still engaged in this Anti-Christian and savage barbarity, "We will not suffer this weak nation to be harassed, and her people to be carried into Slavery and murdered,—we will extend over her the shield of our protection; and, by the law of nations, we demand of you, each and all of you, to cease this cruelty and cowardly injustice to this weak nation." While she makes such a declaration, let her, at the same time, invite all other powers to co-operate with her in this protection, and remonstrate with those who will not.

And while Great Britain, and those States who may unite with her, declare their determination to protect the inhabitants of Africa from being made articles of "merchandise," let them also declare, that they will assume no rights or powers over the territory or people of Africa, but such as are essentially necessary for their protection from the Slave Trade; and that, only so long as such protection is necessary; but will permit

and encourage a Free Trade in the natural and artificial productions of that country.

Such a declaration, on the part of our Government, with the
moral power of the British people to support it, would have a
mighty and a salutary influence on the diplomacy of nations,
especially in regard to this subject. The details of such a
measure are too long, and perhaps not suitable to be given here,
but while we have high expectations from the sincere and re-
solute adoption of such a course, could the Government of this
country be prevailed upon to do so—yet like all moral measures,
its effect would not be instantaneous; perseverance would be
required; and along with this, there should be employed all
other means which are in any way calculated to remove so great
an evil, and which are justifiable on Christian principles.

Africa, with her 100 Millions of Inhabitants, is now almost a
blank in the commercial world, and her people, with the exception of a few hundreds, are sunk in ignorance and idolatry.
We have done much to degrade her—some atonement is, without doubt, required of us.

But it is wisely ordered in the providence of God, that
moral honesty and justice are intimately connected with the
promotion of our secular interests. Thus, by raising Africa
to her place in the scale of nations, she would, to all other
countries, become more valuable in a commercial point of view.

The same may be said of the One Hundred Millions of Inhabitants of British India, referred to by the Aborigines' Society; who, from various causes, are at present very much
oppressed and degraded—some of them in a state of the most
abject slavery; but if elevated, and their industry turned into
a proper channel, it might have a powerful effect in promoting
the Universal Abolition of Slavery and the Slave trade. If,
instead of waste Jungle, and the cultivation of Opium to poison
the Chinese and enrich the unprincipled speculators in that
drug, Cotton and Sugar were cultivated in India, we might soon
become independant of American and Brazilian Slave-grown
articles of that description; and the slaves in those countries,
becoming unprofitable, would soon be Emancipated to provide
for themselves.

Hence, the reference made to India by Mr Thompson, in
advocating the claims of the Aborigines' Society, has been the
means of drawing particular attention to the population of that
vast region; and the beneficial results likely to arise to Commerce and the Abolition of Slavery, by their elevation. It
may be proper here to revert to the fact, that it was *with spe-*

cial reference to the condition of our British Indian fellow-subjects, that the attention of the Glasgow Emancipation Society was first called to the objects of the Aborigines' Society, by Messrs Thompson and Martin, as already noticed. The former found, wherever he went, that, not only from the number of persons in our Eastern Empire claiming the attention of the philanthropist, but from the greatness of the interests involved, and the manner in which these affected the people of this country, there was a general feeling in favour of a separate organization for promoting the welfare of the natives of British India. Mr Thompson's mind became entirely absorbed in the magnitude and importance of this branch of the Aborigines' question, and he was irresistibly led to the conviction, that he ought to confine his labours to the case of India, leaving the general objects of the Aborigines' Society to be taken up by others. A separation between that Society and him, therefore, took place in February last; and a Provisional Committee for the formation of a British India Society having soon after been organized, your Committee were applied to by Mr Thompson, to co-operate in furthering the objects which the Provisional Committee had in view; and having deliberately considered the subject, they were unanimously of opinion, "That this Society may with perfect consistency unite in promoting the objects of the ' British India Society,' and therefore agree to render it all the support which it may be in our power to bestow."

The Provisional Committee having appointed Mr Thompson their Agent, and having received from many places assurances of co-operation, " THE BRITISH INDIA SOCIETY " was ultimately formed in London, on the 6th of July, at a large Public Meeting, of which the Right Hon. Lord Brougham was Chairman; and the Meeting was attended by many of the most distinguished and influential friends of the Slave, from different parts of the country; Abolitionists from the United States of America; Noblemen and Gentlemen long connected with India; several Indian Princes, &c. In the list of its members of Committee, are the names of some of the oldest, most ardent, and devoted friends of the Anti-Slavery cause; and they are actively engaged in diffusing information throughout the kingdom, in order to awaken a general interest on behalf of our oppressed fellow-subjects in the East.

Your Committee have sincere pleasure in stating, that various bodies of Christians have recently resolved, that so far as they are concerned, the interests of Humanity shall not be forgotten. The first of these is, the General Assembly of the

Church of Scotland ; who, at their meeting in May last, came to a unanimous resolution "To petition both Houses of Parliament, that the Government of this country may be pleased to exert their influence with other powers, not only for the extinction of the Slave Trade, which unhappily is still carried on to an awful extent; but likewise for the utter extinction of Slavery itself, as the great cause of the continuance of the Traffic in Slaves."

Several thousand pounds have recently been raised by the Society of Friends, for promoting the improvement of the condition of the Emancipated Negroes in the British Colonies; and a Deputation of members of that body are about leaving for the West Indies, with a view to superintend the application of the Fund, in accordance with the objects which the Society has in view.

The Relief Synod, at its last meeting, was addressed by Mr George Thompson, on the claims of the Inhabitants of British India to the Christian sympathy and effort of the people of this country in their behalf. The thanks of the Synod were given to Mr Thompson, by the Moderator, for his Address, and the following resolution was unanimously passed, viz. :—

"That this Synod tender to Mr George Thompson their warmest expressions of admiration of his character as the advocate of the Negro—but especially at this time, of their gratitude for the manner in which he has this evening interested their minds on behalf of the oppressed and degraded Natives of British India ; and further assure him that they feel their responsibility increased, in consequence of his Address, to use their influence, so far as it extends, to have the miseries of that afflicted people reduced, and the obstacles removed which impede in that land the circulation of the Gospel."

Other denominations of Christians will, your Committee hope, feel themselves called upon still to continue those exertions which, in the struggle recently so auspiciously terminated, essentially contributed to ensure its success; and that while the condition of Slavery is known to exist on the face of the earth, or a human being bought and sold, there will never be wanting those who shall be determined to accomplish, under the Divine blessing, the utter extinction of such Anti-Christian practices.

But whatever may be the determination of others, the Glasgow Emancipation Society, it must be evident, has abundance of labour in prospect. The Society was instituted to promote *the Universal Abolition of Slavery, and the Slave Trade.* It stands pledged, in conjunction with the Aborigines' Society, *to*

Protect the Rights of the Aboriginal Inhabitants in our Colonies : and, with the British India Society, to aid in " *Bettering the Condition of our Fellow-Subjects, the Natives of British India.*" These objects, being of general public interest, your Committee trust they will be sustained in their labours by the continued and increased countenance of the Friends of Freedom.

The Committee cannot close this Report, without briefly adverting to the pecuniary affairs of the Society. The large amount of debt incurred last year is only yet in part paid off. The friends of the cause are therefore earnestly and respectfully entreated to aid, by their contributions, not only in paying off the claims against the Society, but so to replenish their treasury, as to enable the Committee to embrace every opportunity of promoting the welfare of their degraded and oppressed fellow-men.

ERRATUM.—At page 9, line 13 from the top, *for* Mr Gladstone's, *read* Mr Colville's.

SECOND REPORT

OF THE

LASGOW LADIES' AUXILIARY EMANCIPATION SOCIETY.

PRESENTED 1st AUGUST, 1839.

OFFICE-BEARERS.

President,

Mrs WILLIAM WHITE.

Vice-Presidents,

Mrs P. LETHEM, | Mrs D. MACINTYRE, | Mrs Wm. CRAIG.

Treasurer,

Mrs NELSON.

Secretary,

Miss SMEAL.

Committee,

Mrs Blyth,	Mrs Thompson, Campbelton,
Miss Brown,	Mrs Harvie,
Mrs Cochran,	Mrs Hinshelwood,
Miss Craig,	Mrs Martin,
Miss Drummond,	Miss M'Gregor,
Mrs Eadie,	Mrs M'Tear,
Mrs Farie,	Miss Muir,
Miss Ferguson,	Mrs Murray,
Mrs Fletcher,	Mrs Pullar,
Miss Frame,	Miss Smith,
Mrs Robert Frame,	Miss Templeton,
Miss Fullarton,	Mrs William Thompson,
Mrs Gallie,	Mrs Watson,
Miss Gibson,	Miss R. Watson,
Miss J. Gibson,	Mrs Wright.
Miss Hall,	

Honorary and Corresponding Members,

Mrs George Thompson.
Mrs Philleo, (late Miss Crandall.)
Mrs Nathaniel Paul, Albany, New York.
Miss Juliana Tappan, New York.
Mrs A. L. Cox,　　　do.
Mrs H. G. Chapman, Boston.
Mrs James Mott, Philadelphia.
Mrs D. L. Child.
Mrs A. G. Weld.
Miss Hussey, Portland, Maine.
Honourable Mrs Erskine.
Miss Cruickshank, Edinburgh.
Miss Beaumont, Newcastle.
Miss Elizabeth Pease, Darlington.
Mrs Somerville, Dumbarton.

REPORT, &c.

THE Committee deem it unnecessary to submit any detailed account of their proceedings since the date of their last Report, as great publicity has already been given to those proceedings through the medium of newspapers, and other means of information.

They desire, however, to record their gratitude to God, for the truly happy termination of the great national struggle in behalf of the Negroes, one of the noblest struggles in which any nation was ever privileged to be engaged.

The manner in which the Negro population received their entire freedom on the 1st of August last, and their admirable conduct subsequently, have called forth unmingled joy, and have demonstrated that our coloured fellow-subjects are as susceptible of the noblest sentiments, and as capable of discharging the highest duties belonging to citizenship, as they are entitled to personal freedom—which is the gift of God. The great object of freedom for the Slave, having, under the Divine blessing, been attained, the Committee feel that the success which has been granted to their labours, devolves upon them the solemn and interesting task of seeking to promote the education of those, whom they have, in some humble degree, been instrumental in introducing to the privileges and duties of *a free condition:* they will, therefore, embrace every opportunity of imparting the means of intellectual and moral improvement to those whose bonds they have exerted themselves to break. The Committee are happy in being able to state, that an individual of their number is now *on her way* to one of the most important of our Colonies—there to devote herself to the work of *a teacher amongst the liberated population.* She is followed by the best wishes of the Committee, that her life and health may be continued, and that her self-denying efforts may be crowned with abundant success.

The Committee have received from the United States of America, the most encouraging accounts of the progress of the cause of Emancipation; they have forwarded several contributions of articles for sale at various Anti-Slavery Fairs: they have marked with deep interest the struggles, trials, and triumphs, of their Trans-Atlantic sisters, and desire to maintain an uninterrupted correspondence, and to continue and increase their co-operation.

The Committee embrace the present opportunity of tendering an expression of their warmest thanks to all those friends of the cause who have afforded them assistance since their last Report was issued. Amongst those who have kindly helped them with pecuniary means, they feel bound to name the Ladies of Newcastle, from whom a donation of £20 has been received; the Ladies of Darlington, who sent a donation of £10, exclusive of two donations from the esteemed Secretary of the Darlington Association, Miss Elizabeth Pease, amounting together to £15. To those who so promptly and liberally sent contributions to the Ladies' Anti-Slavery Bazaar, they feel that their obligations are eminently due, as the Committee were, in consequence, enabled to realize the means of promoting the cause of the Slave at an interesting and momentous crisis. The Ladies forming the Association at Dumbarton, and the Vale of Leven, are entitled to special thanks, for the strenuous and spontaneous efforts which they made to secure the success of the Bazaar, immediately after they had laboured and contributed in a similar way, in another cause. They also cheerfully and gratefully acknowledge their obligations to those Ministers and other gentlemen, in Glasgow and at a distance, who have forwarded the Committee's plans of usefulness, and have generously undertaken the discharge of duties which the members of the Committee were precluded from performing.

The Committee have recently had their attention called to the condition of the Aboriginal tribes of the British Colonies, and the parts adjacent; and also to the oppressed and suffering circumstances of the many Millions of their native fellow-subjects in India,—*five hundred thousand of whom perished by famine during the past year.* The Gentlemen's Society having extended the basis of *their* Constitution, to embrace the enfranchisement, protection, and improvement of the Coloured inhabitants of the British possessions *at large,* and being now actively engaged in forwarding those objects, *with special reference* to British India, the Committee have resolved to devote a portion of their labours, and the fruits of those labours, to the same work; impressed with a belief, that India is not only a field worthy of the most exalted and persevering enterprise *in itself considered*, but that upon the condition of India, depends, in a great degree, the state of other parts of the world, more particularly *America* and *Africa*, the Slavery and Slave Trade of which countries can only be effectually reached by the *encouragement of free Agricultural industry in our Eastern Empire.*

The Treasurer's Account, an abstract of which is appended to this Report, will exhibit the manner in which the Society's funds have been disbursed. It will be perceived that great expenses have been incurred by the measures which the exigencies of the cause demanded. The Committee's operations having considerably exceeded their receipts; they trust that their friends and subscribers will, with their usual liberality, renew their contributions, and enable the Committee not only to discharge their obligations, but to continue and extend their labours to diffuse information.

The Committee, in the assurance that their friends and fellow-labourers are " *not weary in well-doing,*" have ventured to enter a field of labour, not less arduous, and much more extensive than that in which they have been hitherto permitted to toil and to triumph. They look with confidence for encouragement and support. The miseries of the human race call loudly and imperatively for pity, interference, and prompt relief. Millions of Slaves reach forth their fettered hands to the islands of the *brave* and the *free.*

The mothers and daughters of favoured Scotland have much to be thankful for, and should remember that *the enjoyment of blessings creates corresponding responsibilities.* It is the hope and prayer of the Committee, that the judgment of Him who is the Friend of the destitute and oppressed, may, with reference to each of them, and their respected coadjutors be,—" *She hath done what she could.*"

SUBSCRIPTIONS AND DONATIONS

TO

𝔗𝔥𝔢 𝔊𝔩𝔞𝔰𝔤𝔬𝔴 𝔈𝔪𝔞𝔫𝔠𝔦𝔭𝔞𝔱𝔦𝔬𝔫 𝔖𝔬𝔠𝔦𝔢𝔱𝔶,

From 1st August, 1838, to 1st August, 1839.

A

	£	s	d
David Anderson, . .	1	1	0
James Anderson, . . .	1	1	0
Alexander Anderson, . .	1	1	0
John Anderson, . .	0	10	6
Rev. William Anderson, .	0	10	0
James Anderson, jun., . .	0	10	6
Joseph Affleck, . . .	0	5	0

B

	£	s	d
James Brown, Douglas, per G. Gallie,	1	0	0
Do. do.	0	5	0
Robert Barclay, . .	0	10	0
John Barr, ...	1	1	0
Hugh Brown, ...	1	1	0
Archibald Brown, . .	0	10	6
William Brown, . . .	0	5	0
Moses Brown, . . .	0	5	0
David Boyd, . . .	0	5	0
James Brock, . . .	0	5	0
James Beith, Candleriggs, .	0	5	0
Thomas Binnie, . .	0	7	6
Robert Burns, . . .	0	5	0
Thomas Brown, . . .	0	5	0
Charles Bryson, . .	0	5	0
Peter Bruce, . . .	0	10	6
Henry Bruce, . . .	0	5	0
Andrew Boggie, . . .	0	5	0
William Brodie, . .	1	1	0
Robert Bruce, . . .	0	5	0
William Bankier, . .	1	1	0
Rev. William Brash, .	0	7	6
James Beith, . . .	0	10	6

C

	£	s	d
James Clark, . . .	0	5	0
William Craig, . .	1	1	0
John Croom, . . .	0	5	0
James Cairns, . . .	0	5	0
James Cocker, . . .	0	10	6
William Chisholm, jun., .	0	10	6
Dr. Crawford, Bridgeton,	0	10	0
Andrew Crichton, . .	0	2	6
Allan Clark, . . .	0	5	0
Archibald Cumine & Co.	0	10	6

COLLECTIONS,

	£	s	d
At Thanksgiving Services, Aug. 1st, 1838, viz:—			
Rev. W. Anderson's Chapel, (Joint Service), . .	5	11	2¼
Rev. Dr. Heugh's, do. .	3	4	10½
Old Independent Meeting-House, Oswald Street, .	6	3	0
Reformed Presbyterian Congregation, W. Campbell St.	1	5	8½
Rev. Dr. Wardlaw's Chapel, collected during part of service, ...	1	1	10
Baptist Churches, George St and Portland Street,	1	10	5
Rev. David King's Chapel, .	2	12	0
Rev. Dr. Mitchell's do. .	3	13	1
United Secession Congregation, Hamilton, Rev. Thos. Struthers, . .	1	2	2
Do. do. Dalry, Rev. D. Henderson, . .	0	18	3
Do. do. Stonehouse, Rev. M. M'Gavin, . . .	0	6	0
Do. do. Limekilns, Rev. W. Johnston, . . .	1	8	0
Do. do. Alloa, Rev. W. Frazer, . . .	1	13	0
Do. do. Comrie, Rev. R. T. Walker, . . .	1	16	7
Do. do. Whithorn, Rev. Jas. Gibson, . . .	1	3	0
Do. do. Auchtermuchty, Rev. J. Taylor, . .	1	6	2
Do. do. Stirling, Rev. John Smart, . . .	2	2	2
Do. do. Brechin, Rev. D. Blackadder, . .	1	5	9
Do. do. Wigton, Rev. James Towers, . . .	1	7	0
Do. do. Fenwick, Rev. W. Orr, . . .	0	17	10
Relief Congregation, Campsie, Rev. James Brown, .	0	13	8¼
Do. do. Bellshill, Rev. John Wilson, . .	3	1	5
Do. do. Greenock, Rev. W. Auld, ...	2	14	0

First Relief Congregation, Strathaven, Rev. W. M'Lae,	1 12 6		
Relief Congregation, Ruther-glen, Rev. W. C. Wardrop,	1 0 0	Robert Jameson, . .	1 1 0
Do. do. Ayr, Rev. R. Ren-wick, ...	1 10 0	Rev. John Johnstone, . .	0 5 0
Do. do. Auchtermuchty, Rev. J. Wise, . . .	0 13 0	**K**	
Do. do. Milngavie, Rev. A. M'Naughtan, . . .	0 17 4	Robert Kettle, . . .	1 1 0
Do. do. Kelso, Rev. James Jarvie, ...	0 7 2	A. M'K. Kirkland, . .	0 10 6
Independent Chapel, Paisley, Rev. R. M'Lachlan, . .	0 16 0	Hugh Kennedy, . .	0 5 0
Do. do. Perth, Rev. J. W. Massie, ...	4 0 0	Alexander Kellar, . .	0 5 0
Baptist Congregation, Storie Street, Paisley, . . .	3 3 0	Rev. David King, . .	1 1 0
Old Light Burgher Congrega-tion, New Kilpatrick, Rev.		Rev. Dr. Kidston, .	0 10 0
James Gardner, . .	1 3 6	**L**	
		Robert Laing, . .	0 10 6
D		Andrew Liddell, . .	0 5 0
		William Lang, . .	0 5 0
John Dennistoun, Esq., M.P.,	20 0 0	Thomas Lochhead, . .	0 5 0
George C. Dick, . . .	0 10 6	Thomas Lee, . . .	0 5 0
James Duncan, Mosesfield, .	0 5 0	William Lochead, jun., .	0 5 0
George Duncan, . . .	0 5 0	Patrick Lethem, . . .	5 0 0
		Long and Nicholson, .	0 5 0
E		**M**	
Rev. John Edwards, . .	0 5 0	David Muir, Kilwinning, .	0 5 0
Rev. John Eadie, . .	0 10 0	David M'Arthur, . .	0 2 6
		Mrs Mercer, London, ✠ John Murray, . . .	1 0 0
F		Robert M'Gregor, . .	0 10 6
Friends at Kilwinning, per D. Muir, ...	0 4 0	John Murray, . . .	0 10 6
A Friend, per A. Y., . .	0 1 0	John M'Leod, . . .	0 10 6
Do.	1 1 0	James Muirhead, . .	0 5 0
Finlay and Neilson, . .	0 10 6	Robert M'Kay, . .	0 5 0
John Fyfe, ...	1 1 0	William Milroy, . .	0 5 0
A Friend, ...	0 5 0	Andrew Mitchell, . .	1 1 0
William Ferguson, . .	0 10 6	Anthony M'Keand, . .	1 1 0
James Fleming, . . .	0 10 6	John Maxwell, M. D., .	0 10 0
		Samuel Moir, . .	0 5 0
G		James Milliken, . .	0 5 0
Thomas Grahame, . .	5 0 0	Robert Miller, . . .	0 10 6
John B. Gray, . . .	1 1 0	William Miller, . . .	0 5 0
George Gallie, . . .	0 10 6	Right Rev. Dr. Murdoch, .	0 10 6
Robert Grahame, Whitehill,	5 0 0	Robert Miller, London St.,	0 10 0
William Graham, . .	0 5 0	James More, . . .	0 10 6
William Gilmour, Writer, .	0 5 0	Rev. James M'Tear, . .	0 5 0
Archibald Greenshields, .	0 5 0	Robert Mason, New Lanark,	0 5 0
William Gunn, jun., . .	0 10 6	John M'Gregor, . .	0 10 6
John Galloway, . . .	0 5 0	Peter M'Ara, . . .	0 5 0
Rev. John Graham, . .	0 5 0	William M'Lean, Plantation,	1 1 0
		Robert Miller, Bookseller, .	0 5 0
H		Robert Mathie, . .	0 5 0
		Rev. H. M. M'Gill, . .	0 7 6
W. B. Hodge, . . .	0 10 6	Thomas Muter, . . .	0 5 0
Andrew Harvie, . . .	0 10 6	David Murray, . . .	0 5 0
John Hamilton, Turner, .	0 5 0		
Rev. Dr. Heugh, . .	1 1 0	**N**	
D. A. Hardie, . . .	0 5 0	William Nairn, . .	0 5 0
		P	
		James Proudfoot, . .	0 5 0

S. Pollock,	0	5	0	Donald Macintyre,	1	1	0			
J. Pollock,	0	5	0	A. R. Henderson,	0	5	0			
William P. Paton,	5	0	0	Miss Fullarton,	0	5	0			
Rev. James Paterson,	0	5	0	John A. Fullarton,	0	10	6			
Rev. Thomas Pullar,	0	5	0	Matthew Lethem,	1	1	0	5	4	0

R

T

James Reid, Kilwinning,	0	2	6	Rev. Wm. Thomson,	1	0	0			
John Reid,	0	10	6	Rev. Professor Thomson, Pais-						
J. & C. Risk,	1	1	0	ley,	1	0	0			
Archibald Rigg,	0	5	0	James Turner, Thrushgrove,	0	5	0			

S

W

William Shanks, Johnstone,	1	1	0	William White, Violet Vale,	1	1	0
Rev. Dr Stark, Dennyloanhead,	0	10	6	Archibald Watson,	1	1	0
Alex. Stevenson, Bannockburn,	0	5	0	James Watson,	1	1	0
William Smeal,	0	10	6	Oliver Wingate,	0	10	6
Robert Sanderson,	1	1	0	William Wardlaw,	0	5	0
James Stewart,	1	1	0	Walter Wilson,	0	5	0
William Stewart,	0	5	0	Samuel Wilson,	1	1	0
David Smith,	1	1	0	John Williamson,	0	10	6
F. B. Stuart,	0	5	0	James Wallace,	0	5	0
Thomas H. Slater,	0	5	0	Robert Wylie,	0	5	0
Semple & Co.	1	1	0	William Wotherspoon,	0	5	0
William Strang,	0	5	0	George Watson,	1	1	0
				William Wilson,	0	5	0

Society for Religious Purposes, George Street Chapel.

Rev. Dr Wardlaw,	0	10	6
Thomas Wilson,	0	5	0
J. S. Blyth,	1	1	0
John Gray,	0	5	0

Rev. Dr. Wardlaw,   1 1 0
Rev. Dr. Willis,   1 1 0

Y

Andrew Young,   1 0 0

☞ *Every person subscribing 5s. per annum, is a Member of the Glasgow Emancipation Society, and is entitled to receive a copy of all its publications.—Subscriptions will be thankfully received by* MR JAMES BEITH, *the Treasurer, 59, Hutcheson St.; and by* MR WILLIAM SMEAL, *one of the Secretaries, 161, Gallowgate.*

THE TREASURER OF THE GLASGOW EMANCIPATION SOCIETY.

Dr.

	£	s.	d.
July 31st, 1839.			
To Collection at last Annual Meeting,	9	3	10½
Do. at Thanksgiving Services in the City, for the Abolition of Slavery,	25	12	1¼
Do. at do. in the Country,	39	7	2½
Sale of Tickets for Soiree in the Assembly Rooms,	49	17	0
Collection at Aborigines Public Meeting in George Street Chapel, 6th September, 1838,	4	4	10
Bill from (Dr. Wardlaw's,) "A Friend to Universal Emancipation,"	50	0	0
Interest on Do.,	2	17	8
	52	17	8
Less Legacy Duty,	5	0	0
	47	17	8
Collection at Lecture by Mr Thompson, in George Street Chapel, 14th November, 1838,	3	18	10½
Do. in St. George's Church, Paisley,	2	13	0
Do. (Rev. Dr. Burns's,) in St. George's Church,	4	16	8
For British Emancipator, from Sundries per Rev. John Dunn, Milton Church,	10	0	0
Legacy by the late Mrs Dunn,	6	10	4
Dividend on Accounts due at last Anniversary,	5	4	6
Cash from Society for Religious Purposes in George Street Chapel,	1	12	6
Subscriptions collected by Miss Christina Perry,	116	16	6
Do. do. per William Sneal,	3	7	3¼
Sale of Pamphlets,	66	5	8
Balance due by the Society,			
	£397	7	6½

Cr.

	£	s.	d.
July 31st, 1839.			
By Balance due at last Annual Meeting,	220	13	0
Additional Expences of Delegates to London,	1	0	0
Do. do. of last Petition to Parliament,	0	15	0
Expences at Thanksgiving Services,	0	15	6
Do. of Soiree of Friends of Universal Freedom, in the Assembly Rooms,	40	6	3
Do. of Public Meetings during last year,	12	12	6
Do. of Meetings of Committee,	1	6	6
Do. of Printing 1000 Copies of last Annual Report, Bills, &c., for Public Meetings, Advertising in Newspapers, and for Newspapers transmitted to Correspondents at home and abroad,	89	17	7½
Paid for British Emancipator,	21	13	4
Do. Postages, Carriage, Booking of Parcels, and sundry other sundries, incidental charges,	8	7	10
	£397	7	6½

Glasgow, 1st *August*, 1839.—We have examined the above Account, and the relative Vouchers, and found the same correct; the Balance due by the Society, being Sixty-six Pounds Five Shillings and Eightpence Sterling.

(Signed,)

WM. FERGUSON.
ANDREW YOUNG.

SUBSCRIPTIONS AND DONATIONS

TO THE

Glasgow Ladies' Auxiliary Emancipation Society,

From March, 1837, to 1st August, 1839.

	£	s	d
Mrs Wm. White, Violet Vale,	2	0	0
Collected by do. viz.:—			
A Friend, - - -	1	0	0
Dr. John Black, - -	0	5	0
Thomas Stordy, Carlisle,	0	10	0
Mary Sutton, do.,	0	5	0
Lydia Sutton, Scotby,	0	5	0
Ann Brown, - -	0	5	0
A Friend, - - -	0	1	0
Pamphlets sold by Mrs W.,	0	16	6
Mrs William Craig, -	1	10	6
Collected by do., - -	1	6	0
Do. Mrs Nelson, -	4	19	0
Miss Isabella Smith's Box,	0	14	3
Mrs G. Thomson, Campbelton,			
per Miss Smith, -	0	10	0
Miss E. Brown, -	0	5	0
Anti-Slavery Box, per do.,	0	3	6
Sale of Pamphlets, do., -	1	0	9
Collected by - do., -	1	11	6
Do. do. do., viz.:—			
Miss Terise, - -	0	2	6
Miss J. Terise, -	0	2	6
Mr Wilson, - -	0	5	0
A Friend, - - -	0	1	0
Elizabeth Macauley,	0	5	0
Robert Brownlie, -	0	1	0
Janet Morton, - -	0	1	0
John Caldwell, -	0	1	0
Collected by Misses Gibson, viz.:—			
Mr Naismith, - -	0	10	0
A Friend, - - -	0	2	6
Do., - - -	0	2	6
Miss Smith, - - -	0	5	0
Miss Arnot, - -	0	5	0
Mr Turner, - - -	0	5	0
Miss Wallace, - -	0	5	0
A Friend, - - -	0	2	6
Do., - - -	0	2	6
Do., - - -	0	2	6
Do., - - -	0	2	6

	£	s	d
Misses Gibson's Book, continued :—			
Miss Spencer, - -	0	5	0
Pamphlets sold, -	0	16	10
Collected by Miss Agnes Shaw,	0	17	6
— Miss Mary Hinshelwood,	0	14	6
— Mrs R. Wright, -	1	0	0
Do. do. viz.:—			
Mrs Hunter, - -	0	2	6
Mrs Carr, - -	0	2	6
Mrs M'Nair, - -	0	2	6
Eliza Young, - -	0	2	6
Mrs Jackson, - -	0	2	6
Mrs R. Wright, -	0	5	0
Do. do. -	0	5	0
Janet Wright, - -	0	2	0
Ann Wright, -	0	2	0
Pamphlets sold, -	0	6	9
Collected by Miss J. Frame, viz.:—			
Mr John Craig, - -	0	5	0
Miss Houston, - -	0	5	0
Mrs Russell, - -	0	2	6
Duncan Stewart, -	0	5	0
For Reading Report, -	0	0	7
Collected by Miss Janet Hall,	0	8	8
Do. Miss E. M'Lellan,	0	4	0
Do. Mrs W. Gray,	1	19	6
Pamphlets sold by do.,	1	2	6
Do. do., by John Hardie,	1	7	0
Collected by Miss R. Watson,	0	16	0
— Mrs Cochran, -	1	15	0
Pamphlets sold by do.,	0	6	0
Isabella Greig, -	0	2	6
Collected by do., -	0	14	6
James Kirkland, per do.,	0	2	0
Thomas White, per do.,	0	2	6
Mrs M'Tear, -	0	2	6
Mr James Thomas, Teacher,			
Blackquarry, per do., -	1	0	0
Female Servant, per do.,	0	2	0

Collected by C. Henderson,			
Paisley, - - -	0	16	0
Publications sold by do.,	0	4	6
Friends at Paisley, per Robert Eaglesim, viz.:—			
Mrs Kerr, Oakshaw Street,	0	5	0
Mrs Pollock, Maxwelton,	0	2	6
Mrs Connell, Wellmeadow St.,	0	1	6
Mrs Whitehill, do.,	0	2	6
Mrs Poulson, High Street,	0	3	0
Collected by Miss Templeton, viz. :—			
Miss Graham, - -	0	15	0
J. Craig, - - -	0	7	6
Mrs Rennie, - -	1	0	0
J. Lindsay, - - -	0	3	0
Mrs Lancaster, -	0	2	6
W. Gray, - - -	0	1	0
Mrs Alexander, - -	0	15	0
W. C., - - -	0	10	0
Mrs Stewart, -	0	5	0
Mrs Simpsom, - -	0	6	0
J. B., - - -	0	2	0
Catherine W. Spence, -	0	5	0
Mrs Russell, -	0	5	0
Miss M'Farlane, -	0	2	6
Miss E. Templeton, -	0	2	0
Mrs Campbell, -	0	8	0
Mrs Martin, Strathmiglo,	0	2	6
Elizabeth Alexander, -	0	2	6
Miss Brodie, - - -	0	5	0
Mrs Crichton, - -	0	3	0
Three Friends, - -	0	5	0
Mrs M'Nair, - -	0	3	0
Pamphlets sold by Miss T.,			
Jane Smeal, jun., - -	1	0	0
Publications sold by do.	3	7	6
Collected by do., viz.:—			
Miss Pease, Darlington,	10	0	0
Do. do. do.	5	0	0
Do. do. for 50 Reports,	1	5	0
Mrs John Wigham, Edinburgh, for "Wrongs of Africa,"	2	16	6
Miss M. B. Tuckey, Cork, do.	4	0	0
Misses Smith, Græme Street,	1	12	6
Mrs Jackson, - -	0	2	6
John Craig, Stockwell Street,	0	10	6
Hugh Fulton, - -	0	5	0
Miss M'Gregor, - -	0	5	0
Do. per Box, -	0	5	5
Mary Marchbank, -	0	5	0
Agnes M'Leod, -	0	5	0
James Crowther, -	0	2	6
Sarah Wells, - -	0	5	0
D. A. Hardie, - -	0	7	6
Agnes Sutherland, - -	0	2	6
Miss Crawfurd, Langside,	5	0	0
Mrs Thomas Gray, per R. Miller, London Street,	0	5	0
For Expenses of Ladies' Petition, per do., -	0	4	1
Mrs Robert Miller, - -	1	1	0
Mrs Ballantine, 5, Buchanan Street, - - -	0	2	6
Mrs Cairnduff, Stewarton, -	0	5	0
A Friend, - -	0	1	0

Jane Smeal's Book, continued :—			
Miss E. Stark, Dennyloanhead,	0	8	0
Reports sold, - -	0	2	0
Mrs Kaye, Russell Street,	0	2	6
Robert Dougall, - -	0	2	6
Miss C. Findlater, -	0	5	0
Mrs White, Adelphi Street,	0	7	6
A Friend, (H. E.,)	0	1	0
James Collins, Tradeston, -	0	4	0
Mrs Collins, do. -	0	2	6
Mrs Stephen, Largs. -	0	2	6
Robert Gray, Denmill, -	0	2	6
Mrs M'Lay, Strathaven, -	0	2	6
Mrs Campbell, do., -	0	5	0
Sale of Tracts at Milnathort,	0	8	0
Friend at Old Kilpatrick, per J. Murray, -	0	4	0
A Friend, (J. F.,) -	1	5	0
Mrs Andrew Miller, -	0	3	0
Helen Mulcaster, -	0	2	6
A Friend, (M. B.,) -	1	0	0
Mrs William Thompson, -	0	3	0
Robert Hepburn, -	0	2	6
Misses E. & C. Paton, -	0	5	0
Andrew Robertson, -	0	10	0
Robert Thallon, -	0	5	0
James Grindlay -	0	5	0
David Gilmour, -	0	5	0
Patrick Gilmour, -	0	5	0
Mrs Steel, -	0	5	0
James Wotherspoon, -	0	7	6
David Black, -	0	7	6
James Armstrong, -	0	0	6
Andrew Mouat, jun., -	0	5	0
John Angus, - -	0	3	6
Thomas Aucott, -	0	2	6
James Marshall, - -	0	5	0
William Greig, -	0	1	0
Miss M. Browning.	0	5	0
Elizabeth Smeal, -	0	2	6
Mrs R. Rettie, - -	0	5	0
Miss Agnes Barlas, - -	0	2	6
Sarah Dodds, per G. Gallie,	0	5	0
William Miller, Blackfriar's st.	0	5	0
Mrs James Clark, - -	0	2	6
Mrs Andrew Harvie, -	0	5	0
Do. for Publications sold,	0	11	0
Friends, per Mrs H., -	0	8	0
Miss Adam, - -	0	5	0
Janet Wright, Græme Street,	0	5	0
George Cruden, - -	0	2	6
George M'Kinlay, -	0	5	0
Robert Thom, - -	0	10	0
A Friend, - - -	0	1	0
A. Wotherspoon, -	0	0	6
Gabriel Anderson, -	0	2	6
John Shaw, - -	0	2	6
Andrew Henderson, -	0	2	6
Miss Ferguson, - -	0	5	0
Miss H. Ferguson, - -	0	5	0
Mrs Thomson, Paisley, per do.,	0	2	6
Mrs R. G. Maxwell, -	0	5	0
James Fleming, Cowcaddens,	0	5	0
Mrs John Duncan, Argyle St.	0	2	6
J. C. Wilson, - -	0	5	0
James Smith, - -	0	5	0
Claud Turner, - -	0	2	6

Jane Smeal's Book, continued:—			
Mrs N. M'Gilp, - -		10	0
Do. for Publications sold,	0	9	0
Robert Frame, - -		10	0
Mrs Robert Frame, -	0	2	6
Ann Lee, - - -		5	0
Mrs A. Liddell, - -		5	0
Miss M'Murrich, per R. Kettle,		10	0
Andrew Reid, per R. S.,		1	0
Elizabeth Maxwell, ..		5	0
A Friend, - - -		4	6

Jane Smeal's Book, continued:—			
Mrs Reid, - -		0	2	6
Mrs Bland, - - -		0	5	0
Lady at Kirkintilloch, per Mrs Andrew Marshall, -		1	0	0
Mrs D. Macintyre, -		0	5	0
Miss S. Craig, - -		0	2	6
Mrs Gentle, - -		0	2	6
Mrs P. Lethem, - -		0	5	0
Miss Robertson, St. Enoch Square, per do., .		1	0	0

∗ *All Subscribers of 2s. 6d. and upwards per annum, are Members of the Ladies' Emancipation Society. Subscriptions and Donations will be gratefully received by the Treasurer, or Secretary ; and by any Member of the Committee.*

THE TREASURER OF THE GLASGOW LADIES' AUXILIARY EMANCIPATION SOCIETY.

Dr.

	£	s.	d.
July 31st, 1839.			
To Donation from Darlington Ladies' Society, per Miss Pease,	£10	0	0
Do. from Aberdeen Ladies' Society, per Mr George Thompson,	12	10	0
Do. from Newcastle Ladies' Society, per Mrs Richardson,	20	0	0
Collection at Meeting in Rev David King's Chapel, to Address the Queen,	4	10	4
Proceeds of Anti-Slavery Bazaar in the Monteith Rooms,	328	15	6½
Do. do. at Kilmarnock,	87	0	0
Contributions from Friends of Emancipation in the Country,	8	15	4½
Amount of Subscriptions, Donations, Sales of Miss Grimke's Appeal, the "Wrongs of Africa," Annual Report, &c.	116	2	10½
Balance Due by the Society,	25	17	8½
	£613	11	10

Cr.

	£	s.	d.	£	s.	d.
July 31st, 1839.						
By Balance due the Treasurer at last Report,				£0	5	1
Donations to Glasgow Emancipation Society, viz.:—						
June 6th, 1837,	£10	0	0			
July 29th, do.,	12	10	0			
November 13th, do.,	20	0	0			
July 31st, 1838,	185	2	10½*	227	12	10½
Expenses of Ladies' Petition to the Queen,				86	11	5
Do. of Bazaar at Glasgow and Kilmarnock,				170	4	8
Do. of Committee Meetings, of Annual Meeting, 1837, and Meeting to Address the Queen,				4	19	7
Do. of Advertising, and for Newspapers sent to Correspondents at home and abroad,				8	13	8
Do. of Printing Circulars, 1500 copies; First and 1st and 2d editions of "The Wrongs of Africa," each 1000 copies,				95	12	5½
Paid for 500 Copies Angelina Grimke's Appeal,				9	7	6
Do. for Howitt's "Colonization and Christianity," for use of Committee,				0	9	0
Outlay for Cuts to Anti-Slavery Fair at Boston, United States,				2	10	4
Do. for Ladies' Bazaar at New				5	3	5
Postages and Carriage of Parcels,				2	1	10
				£613	11	10

GLASGOW, 1st *August*, 1839.—We have this day examined the above Account, and compared the Vouchers produced, and found it correct; the Balance due by the Society being £25 17s. 8½d.

(Signed,)

WM. FERGUSON.
ANDREW YOUNG.

* These sums are acknowledged in the Gentlemen's Report for last year.

APPENDIX.

No. I.

SPEECHES DELIVERED AT THE FIFTH ANNIVERSARY OF THE GLASGOW EMANCIPATION SOCIETY.

(Reprinted, with a few corrections, from the GLASGOW ARGUS.)

THE Annual Meeting of this Society was held in the Rev. Dr. Wardlaw's Chapel on Thursday evening, the 1st of August, being the Anniversary of the Abolition of Slavery in the British Colonies. To give readers at a distance an idea of the nature of this Society, we give the following statement of its objects, as laid down in the advertisement calling the meeting:—
"The Glasgow Emancipation Society has for its objects, the Universal Abolition of Slavery and the Slave Trade—the Protecting of the Rights of the newly Emancipated and Aboriginal Classes in the British Colonies —and the Improving of the Condition of our Fellow-Subjects, the NATIVES of BRITISH INDIA; objects alike worthy of the support of the Christian, the Patriot, and the Philanthropist."
We observed on the platform around the Chair, which was occupied by Dr. Wardlaw, Major-General Briggs, George Thompson, Esq., Rev. Dr. Heugh, Rev. Messrs. Anderson, Baird (of Paisley), Harvey, and M'Tear; Thomas Grahame, W. P. Paton, J. M'Leod, one of the Magistrates of Gorbals; D. Macintyre, G. Watson, H. Langlands, J. Murray, W. Smeal, A. M'Keand, J. Reid, J. Beith, J. S. Blyth, W. Ferguson, and G. Thorburn, Esqrs.; Drs. Maxwell and Weir, and other friends of the Anti-Slavery cause.
Dr. WARDLAW, in opening the business, said it afforded him the greatest pleasure to be present on this interesting occasion—the Anniversary of the Abolition of Slavery in the British Colonies, as well as the Annual Meeting of the Glasgow Emancipation Society—though the pleasure would have been enhanced had he been allowed to be a silent spectator of the proceedings, and a silent listener to that information, important as he was sure it would be, which they were that night to receive. It was his purpose to have made a few remarks, retrospective as well as prospective, in reference to the cause in which they were engaged; but, in order to give full time to the reading of the Reports, and the addresses of the various speakers, in which all the points he might have referred to would be touched upon, he would abstain from doing so. They would no doubt receive much valuable information from an esteemed and valued friend (Mr Thompson) whom they all delighted to see once more among them. It was his (Dr. W.'s) earnest desire and prayer, that he might prove equally triumphant in the cause in which he was now embarked, as in that to which he had for so

many years devoted his talents and his energies. (Cheers.) The Rev. Doctor then stated that letters, in excuse of absence, had been received from John Dennistoun, Esq., M.P., the Rev. Drs. Thomson and Burns, Paisley, and Johnston, Limekilns. The letter from Mr Dennistoun, which was read to the Meeting, expressed his regret that attendance upon his duties in Parliament prevented him presiding at the Anniversary, and that Mr Oswald was also kept back from a similar cause. The Chairman said Mr Dennistoun was fully entitled to the notice of having his letter read, not merely as being their representative, but as being a very liberal contributor to their funds. (Cheers.)

JOHN MURRAY, Esq., then read the Report for the year. It represented the prospects of the Emancipationists in a favourable light, and vindicated the character of the West Indian Negro population. It asserted that the enfranchised blacks had been peaceable in the extreme, that militia or police were not required in the West India Islands, that the Negroes are industrious where well rewarded, and that, where not well rewarded, they had a right to withhold their labour, or take it to a better market. A great deal of finesse had been put into requisition by the Planters, in order to make the people of this country believe that there would be a deficiency of crop; but this would be speedily effaced. So soon as a fair value was put upon labour, the plantations would be better cultivated than before. The Report then went on to notice the miseries of the Hill Coolies of Hindostan, imported into British Guiana under the "Gladstone Order in Council." After recapitulating some of the horrors endured by these people, which we have already detailed in our columns, it observes that the unfeeling remark of an attorney on one of the estates was that the misery endured was necessary to the "Apprentice's acclimation." The scene was then changed to Antigua, where full freedom had been enjoyed for five years. In that island the crops had equalled those of the last five years of slavery. Society was rapidly progressing. Schools and churches were being built in great numbers, and education was eagerly sought after. Such was the result of complete Emancipation in Antigua. The principle of Emancipation was, moreover, spreading widely. The Spanish slaveholders of Cuba were becoming alarmed; the French Institute had offered a prize for the best essay on the subject. Still what had been done was only an experiment. The Aborigines of our other colonies were to be protected, and their energies called forth, and the Committee of the Glasgow Emancipation Society had agreed to join efforts with the society formed for the advancement of those distant tribes and nations now subjected to British sway. Notwithstanding the example of England, the slave trade was still carried on to a shameful extent, and it was proposed to hold a conference of Anti-Slavery Delegates, assembled from all parts of the world, in London, in order to devise means by which the accursed traffic might be suppressed. Justice would in this case be profitable. Civilized Africa would become a mart for British manufactures. In the same way good government would enable India to consume and to pay for the commodities of this country. Instead of raising opium to poison the Chinese, cotton might be produced on the fertile plains of Hindostan, so as to strike a blow at American slavery, never to be withstood or recovered. With these views the Glasgow Emancipation Society had joined cause with the British India Society established in London, and they trusted that they would be enabled to go forward till Slavery and the Slave Trade were banished from the face of the earth.

Mr Murray next read extracts of a letter from the pen, we believe, of W. L. Garrison of Boston, in which the most cheering prospects were held out for the abolition cause. Mr Garrison, in his own peculiarly fervent language, contrasts the position of the friends of Universal Freedom, in 1829 and in 1839. At the former period there was but one individual in wide America to lift up his voice in behalf of the slave; now there are hundreds of thousands engaged in the cause of liberty. In 1829 there was not one society with Emancipation for its object; now there are two thousand. In 1829 there was not a periodical publication that ventured to advocate the native rights of the black man; now there were scores of such works. Ten years ago, that scourge of the *coloured* race, and most inhuman association, the American Colonization Society, was flourishing like a green bay tree; now it was held in such mean esteem as that few were to be found to do it reverence.

The Report, with Mr Garrison's letter, received the hearty applause of the meeting.

Mr WILLIAM SMEAL then read an abstract of the accounts of the Society for the past year, from which it appeared that £154 of debt had been paid off. The same gentleman read a Report from the Ladies' Auxiliary Emancipation Society, in which a strong appeal is made to the Christian feeling of the Mothers and Daughters of favoured Scotland, in aid of the cause of education in our Colonial possessions; and concludes by expressing a confident expectation, that the friends and subscribers to the Society will, with their wonted liberality, sustain the Committee in their efforts to diffuse information, in reference, particularly, to British India.

The Rev. Dr. HEUGH proposed that the Reports now read be adopted, printed, and circulated, under the direction of the Committee. They were to bear in mind that what had been read was only an abstract of the Reports. He regretted that he did not perfectly hear them; but he was sure that they would be very unlike all such documents that had gone before them, if they were not stored with an excellent supply of important facts and reasonings; and he was sure that sending these abroad over Glasgow, could not but give an impulse to the cause they all had so much at heart. He felt, and every member of the society must feel along with him, that they were under great obligations to the uncommon zeal, indefatigable labours, and very distinguished ability of their highly respected Secretaries, and for the pains they took in preparing these documents. (Cheers.) He should consider it absolutely criminal were he that night to make a speech, considering what they had already heard, and what they were yet to hear from the lips of one who had so often instructed and delighted them, and who would do so over again; and what they were also to hear from the lips of the gallant General, who had made himself singularly well acquainted with Indian affairs, and the all but incredible, he might say, absolutely incredible, condition of that country, were it not supported by evidence to which no mind could refuse assent. (Cheers.) They should bear in mind that they were only in the outset of their exertions, and should recollect the deplorable fact which Mr Buxton had made too evident in his book—a book he would recommend to the reading of all— that the Slave Trade was not in any degree diminished, but had additional horrors connected with it, and was in three-fold greater activity at this day, partly through British capital, than when Thomas Clarkson first commenced his career of benevolence. (Hear, hear.) Mr Buxton believes that no trade, however immoral, however debasing its character, or monstrously inhuman it may be, if it only insure a return of from thirty to forty per cent. can be put down, but is sure to drive its way, in spite of all the penalties which civil law can interpose to prevent it. (Cheers.) If he was not mistaken, this trade brought a return of 130 per cent. into the pockets of its inhuman conductors. (Hear.) They were, therefore, only in the outset of their exertions; but he trusted they were in the outset, and that they would go forward in the good work. (Cheers.) If any thing was calculated to animate them more than another, next to the justice of the cause, and their impulses of humanity towards the oppressed and their oppressors, he would say that the splendid success of the cause in America, as shown by the heart-stirring document read from the pen of Garrison, was well calculated to influence every mind present, and to excite us to redoubled exertion. (Cheers.)

The Rev. Mr Anderson simply seconded the Resolution, which was carried unanimously.

The Rev. Mr Baird of Paisley moved the next Resolution :—

" That the thanks of this Meeting are due to those Ministers and Congregations, who last year so cordially responded to the recommendation of this Society, both with respect to the observance of a time of Thanksgiving for the Abolition of Colonial Slavery, and the Collections in aid of our Funds ; and this Meeting cherishes the hope, that these Friends will continue to co-operate with us in the great cause of Human Freedom."

The recommendation referred to in the motion he had just read, and for the purpose thus stated, was, he observed, well entitled to the cordial response which it had so generously and so gladly received.— Most of the towns and villages and districts of the western neighbourhood of this city, gave that response in the most cordial manner. It is true there were many—nay, it may be said, that with a few honourable exceptions, there were nearly all of the ministers of a certain denomination who had stood aloof from this struggle, carried on so long and so hotly between the friends and foes of freedom ; and it is quite possible that many of them, though their hearts might rejoice with us in the result of the contest, might yet feel it awkward in taking part with the various sections of the Christian community in public thanksgiving, in reference to the issue of a struggle which they had aided so little, and with which they had sympathised still less. (Hear, hear.) Yet there were honourable exceptions ; and it is with pleasure I say, that this recommendation was complied with in the town of Paisley in the most fraternal manner, by ministers of all denominations. (Cheers.) I have great pleasure in saying, that the ministers of the Established Church in that town, during the time of my residence there, have been, all and each of them, with a very rare exception indeed, the warm and steadfast friends of this cause, not merely in the hour of its ascendancy, but at a time when to stand forth in its defence subjected those who did so to deep odium and bitter reproach. (Cheers.) I may state, in reference to this matter, and I have pleasure in doing so, as a pleasing exposition of the state of matters in other places, that on the afternoon of the 1st of August, last year, Mr Brewster preached an appropriate sermon, in the Abbey church, to a crowded audience ; and on the evening of that day a crowded assembly was convened in St. George's church, to offer up thanksgiving to Almighty God. The devotional services with which the meeting commenced were performed by Dr Thomson of the Relief ; Dr Burns and myself delivered addresses from the pulpit, and the services were concluded by Mr M'Nair of the Abbey church ; and there were not fewer than five or six of the Established ministers of the place present. This was an occasion well fitted to unite all hearts, and to lead the friends of humanity and religion to offer up thanksgiving to God, who had, in such a very signal way, overpowered the opposition of men to a cause so glorious—who had made the wrath of man to praise him, and who had restrained the remainder thereof. It was fitting that they, the friends of humanity in that place, and in all other places, should, on such an occasion, say devoutly and publicly, " This also cometh forth from the Lord of Hosts, who is wonderful in counsel, and excellent in working." Yes! it was He who inspired the friends of this high and holy cause with that zeal which carried them nobly on in the face of appalling difficulties, and frequently apparently insurmountable difficulties—who sustained them amid the dispensation of frequent and sometimes apparently ruinous defeat—who gave them fresh energy at every renewed onset to look unshrinking on the power of their enemies, and to battle corruption in her strongholds, till every fortress gave way—till at last the accursed system fell in a moment —fell unexpectedly—fell, as if smitten by the thunderbolt of an unseen but Almighty arm. (Cheers.) The system thus overthrown, I need not say, was a system of atrocious injustice. (Hear.) The nature of civil association requires that those who place themselves under its protection, and who enjoy its many privileges, should relinquish a portion of their individual rights, in order that the good of all may be secured, and the protection and happiness of all promoted ; but the institution of Slavery requires that the Slave should relinquish every right which is dear to man —that he should not only relinquish these, but relinquish them for the sole and exclusive advantage of another—who is to task him as a brute, and as a brute drive him to his labour by the sound of the lash. Is he a man ?— he is told he has no property even in himself ; his flesh, blood, and bones are the property of another. (Loud cheering.) Is he a parent ?—his children are not his own. Is he a husband ?—his wife is not his own ; and the tender relation that binds them to each other, may be severed in a moment, not at the fiat of the Creator, but by the caprice and tyranny of his fellow-men. (Loud cheers.) And what are the fruits such a system may be expected to yield ? Is there any thing so revolting in cruelty— is there any thing so loathsome in licentiousness—is there any thing so base in vice—is there any thing so fiend-like in violence—is there any thing so hostile in all its influences, to the progress of religion, and the triumphs of the gospel, which it may not be expected to yield, as its native and proper growth? (Cheers.) And in point of fact, are not these the very fruits which it has yielded? In every clime and era of the world, it has been the parent of crime, of ruin, desolation, woe, and death. (Cheers.) And under present circumstances, when the barren tree is rooted up—when the towering pyramid of evil is laid prostrate—when the compact system of crime is dissolved—when a way is opened up for the diffusion of the blessings of freedom and religion, to a long-suffering and much-injured race—when a mighty impulse is given to the movement of this noble cause in every land, where the bitter cup of Slavery is still drunk, and its heavy chain is still dragged—shall we not rejoice? Does it not become the friends of religion to assemble and give thanks to God— did it not become them then, does it not become them still to rejoice—to rejoice that, notwithstanding the wiles of human policy, and the force of human tyranny, the Lord reigneth, and that every system of iniquity shall at last be laid prostrate before Him ? (Cheering.) I have just to notice, in one word, that this motion expresses the hope that its friends will continue to co-operate in the great cause of human freedom. Oh, how much need is there still of this co-operation ! When we reflect upon the details this night laid before us in the Report—(Hear)—when we think of one thousand human beings still torn from the land of their birth—a land so long trodden down in ruin by the cupidity and tyranny of civilized man— a thousand human beings every day murdered, or sold into Slavery ! there is, indeed, much land to be possessed—there is many a bitter cup of Slavery yet to be dashed to the ground—many woes to be redressed. (Hear, hear.) If we look to the state of things in Europe, there, in defiance of solemn treaties, and of treaties into which those powers were induced to enter by large remunerative grants from the taxes of this country, the flag of many of the maritime states of Europe is still unfurled to protect the increasing and uninterrupted horrors of the African Slave-Trade: the star-bespangled banner of Republican America is red with blood—though we have reason to rejoice, from the accounts read this evening, that that foul stain will yet be wiped away, and that the echoes of the loud shout of her freedom that comes ever and anon over the western wave, shall yet not be stained with the groans of captive millions, and turned to bitter mockery and loathsome hypocrisy. (Cheers.) And turn we to our own empire in the East. Many of us foolishly imagined that the time had come when every yoke was broken in our own dominions; but it is not so. In a Bill introduced in 1833, and which passed through the Commons House, for the opening up of the India trade, there was a clause which went to give liberty to the millions in a state of Slavery in the Indian empire; but when it reached the House of Lords, true to their character of obstructives, they threw it out. (Hear.) And shall we permit that clause to be continually thrust out ? Shall the friends of humanity not rally around the millions of our fellow-men kept in Slavery, and continue to give our aid, our sympathies, our energies, and our consecrated talents to a cause so great and so noble? (Cheers.) Yes, my friends, I trust we will do so till the great trumpet of civil and religious liberty has been blown in the ear of every human being, and every captive ear has rejoiced in its heart-thrilling sound. (Cheers.)

Bailie M'LEOD seconded the Resolution, which was carried unanimously.

The Rev. Mr HARVEY of Calton, proposed the next Resolution:—

" That this meeting rejoices in the formation of the London Society for promoting Universal Abolition ; that we renew the expression of our fervent desire for the success of our Anti-Slavery brethren and sisters in America; and whilst, in common with the friends of humanity everywhere, we deplore the continued existence and increased activity of the traffic in human beings, we feel called upon to reiterate our conviction, that so long as Slavery is suffered to exist in any quarter of the globe, the Slave Trade will never be effectually put down—and therefore resolve, under the Divine blessing, to promote, to the utmost of our power, the Universal Extinction of Slavery."

Mr HARVEY said, I regard the cause in which we are engaged as one truly sacred, and involving alike the interests, the honour, and the happiness of mankind. The Christian can know no distinction of colour or class. If he has imbibed the spirit of his Divine Master, and has his heart thoroughly imbued with the principles of his religion, he must admit that God made of one blood, though not of one colour, all who dwell on the face of the earth. And every enlightened individual, though he has not imbibed the spirit of Christ, must venerate man as man, and not on account of some of those adventitious circumstances which he may have obtained in consequence of the peculiar situation in which Providence has ordered his lot. (Cheers.) I have always thought that the sacred injunction in Holy Writ has not been sufficiently attended to on this point. We read that honour is due to kings, and I fully admit that honour is due to those high in office, but at the same time, there is recorded in the same book, the injunction " honour all men." Honour them as men—(Great cheering)—honour them because they possess a common humanity with ourselves, though perhaps not so highly favoured as we. Yet recollect, that were we in their circumstances, and not more favoured of Providence than they, our lot would have been theirs, and we would have been smarting under the very ills they undergo. (Cheers.) Is it not enough to make us blush for the privileges of freedom men enjoy, when, instead of employing their superior advantages for the good of their fellow-creatures, they employ their influence for the purpose of debasing, injuring, stealing, and insulting their fellow-men. (Cheering.) Mr H. then proceeded to speak in reference to the various clauses of the Resolution. He observed that they had reason to rejoice that in the metropolis the question of universal abolition had been taken up by a society lately instituted there. We cannot, however, he proceeded, give our London brethren the credit of originating the present movement. I believe that the idea of originating this great object was first mooted in Glasgow. (Hear.) A number of years ago societies were formed in this country; but we are, nevertheless, glad that the subject has been taken up in England, and, above all, in London, where they have more influence with those in authority, and more extensive communication with other parts of the world than we have; and therefore the influence they can bring to bear on this cause will be more directly and more immediately felt than in any other part of the kingdom. (Hear.) After expressing a hope that the London Society would pursue their object with energy and zeal, Mr H. referred to the progress of the cause of emancipation in America. They had said at their meetings years ago, that, if the Americans once took up this subject, it would go on with gigantic strides; and, though the cry of Liberty was at first heard amid blood and crime, yet he trusted they would hear no more of such outrages—that they would hear no more of the brick-bat, of mobs, or of Lynch-law to crush infant liberty. (Cheers.) Mr H. next referred to the slave trade. They had believed that an occasional pirate was now and then seen upon the coast of Africa, engaged in this horrible traffic; but till of late they had no idea of the extent to which the atrocious trade was carried. Instead of being diminished, it existed to a greater degree than ever, and with more cruelty than ever. Formerly the traffic in slaves was regulated by statutes; and, as a consequence of its being recognized by the law of the land, those statutes extended some kind of protection to the captured slave; but now the trade is carried on by desperadoes, who run double risks—who are liable to be seized as pirates, and therefore they were compelled to resort to cruelties formerly unknown. (Hear.) They have been known, when pursued, to stow hundreds of their victims into casks, and throw them into the sea, in order that the proofs of the horrid traffic in which they were engaged might not be found against them. (Hear.) After dwelling upon the necessity for crushing the slave trade, which, he observed, could never be done by treaties, but only by abolishing slavery, and thus stopping the demand for slaves, Mr H. impressively called upon his audience, by every motive which humanity and religion could furnish, to devote their entire energies to the promotion of the great and holy cause in which they were engaged, and concluded by moving the Resolution.

Dr. MAXWELL seconded the Resolution, which was also carried unanimously.

The CHAIRMAN (the Rev. Dr. WARDLAW,) in introducing MAJOR-GENERAL BRIGGS to the meeting, stated that the gallant General had spent thirty-two years in India—had administered the affairs of the Government in several provinces—had travelled over almost every part of British India—was the author of an elaborate and able work on the Land Tax of India, and a member of the Committee of the *London British*

India Society. He (Dr. W.) was most glad to invite their attention to so distinguished a coadjutor in the cause of humanity.

MAJOR-GENERAL BRIGGS then rose, amidst much applause, and said:— After a long and dark night of ignorance, light is beginning to burst upon us from its natural quarter, and the condition of eighty millions of our fellow-subjects in the East has begun to attract notice in England. Those millions have been shut out from our attention by their vast distance, and from our sympathies by the great ignorance which has pervaded this country regarding them. Within late years, some of our countrymen have published their travels amongst these people ; and in giving lively pictures of their habits, so different from our own, yet apparently so simple and so primitive, they have excited much interest. To admire the people of India, it is only necessary to have lived among them as I have done for more than thirty years, and to have studied their character through their own languages—(Cheers)—and I defy any one who has done so, to look back on them without kindliness, or to think on them without feelings of regard. Before I speak of the condition of the country, I shall therefore say a few words respecting the character of the Natives. The late Rammohun Roy, who visited you some years ago, affords a fair sample of a Hindoo of the Bengal Presidency ; and the Prince of Oude, who is now in London, and who passed through Glasgow about this time last year, is a favourable specimen of a Mohammedan native gentleman from Upper India. (Cheers.) The Parsees of Bombay seem, perhaps, to exhibit stronger proofs of attachment to our countrymen, than the natives of any other portion of the East. They are an intelligent and an enterprising race, as may be supposed, when I tell you that some, who are in frequent correspondence with Sir Charles Forbes, became possessed of great wealth from slender beginnings. One of these, in particular, commenced his career by buying and selling empty bottles, till, from a small shop, he extended his concern to a warehouse. He afterwards engaged in other business, and eventually left off his mercantile pursuits in 1830. In that year he addressed a letter in English to his friend, Sir C. Forbes, which evinces an elegant as well as a devout mind, and to parts of which I shall now refer you. The paragraphs I allude to are as follow. The first has reference to a letter from Sir Charles Forbes to him, and the second to the sudden death of a mutual friend, Mr James Forbes, a partner in the house of Forbes & Co. :—

Extracts from a Letter dated 5th Jan., 1830, from Jenesetjee Jujubehyr, to Sir Charles Forbes, Bart., M. P.

" I feel greatly obliged by your kind expressions and good opinion of me, which are indeed highly flattering. I beg to assure you, my honoured Sir, that if I at all merit the encomiums which you have so profusely lavished on me, it is for the most part to be ascribed to the advantage I have derived from studiously adhering to the friendly and valuable advice which you condescended to give me on your departure from Bombay.

" It is with feelings of the deepest sorrow I take my pen to condole with you on the decease of our much-esteemed friend, Mr James Forbes, who met his death on the 2d ultimo, by an accident, producing a fracture of the skull, from which he shortly after expired. Having had the honour of great intimacy and friendship with him, I had frequent occasions to witness his nobleness of heart and social virtues. It is therefore by no means surprising, that your good self, as well as his other friends, require extraordinary fortitude on this melancholy occasion.

" But, as there are none exempted, in this transitory world, from discharging this debt of nature, however severe the loss may be, the only alternative left for us is an entire resignation to the will of Providence, whose dispensations are always just, and unquestionably for our ultimate good." (Cheers.)

This good man, in the possession of considerable wealth, has lately given £10,000 sterling to endow a native hospital for his countrymen in Bombay—(Cheers)—and trusts that the Government will add the interest annually of a similar amount, which has been done. Since that he has, in addition, contributed £1000 more to aid in building the hospital. In a letter on the subject, written 4th September, 1838, he adds the following postscript:—

" If you find any difficulty to get the sanction of the Court for 6 per cent. (on the £10,000,) in that case I give you full discretionary power to increase my donation as you may deem proper to attain the object I have in view, for securing 6000 Rupees (£600) per annum to this institution for ever." (Cheers.)

The son of Jenesetjee, the well-known ship-builder in Bombay, who died, leaving a very small fortune, has lately sent two of his sons to the care of Sir Charles, in London, to be placed under the tuition of a clergyman in that vicinity, in order that they may be well grounded in the English language, and in mathematics. They are then to be sent to the English building docks, to study the science of naval architecture, before they return to their own country. In Madras, the late Ram Raja, a Brahmin, whom I had an opportunity of placing in the highest responsible judicial station in Mysore, was by no means inferior, in point of European acquirements, to Rammohun Roy, and wrote during his lifetime an interesting and learned work on the architecture and sculpture of the Hindoos, adorned with a vast number of plans and plates, indicating a high state of the art of building at a remote period of antiquity. This essay has been published in the transactions of the Royal Asiatic Society. So much for their men ; now let us say a word of their literature. Those who are learned in Sanscrit have pronounced some portions of the Ramayan and the Mahabharat, two of their heroic poems, to be not inferior to the Iliad and the Odyssey ; and every day is developing histories which have not yet been translated, among the Hindoos. The Mohammedan historians are as faithful, if not so copious, as Livy or Tacitus. The commentaries of Baber, written by himself, like those of Cæsar, are little, if at all inferior to them in simplicity, and abound in reflections, the result of an acute and observing mind. With their kingdoms, the patrons of their literature have departed, and all composition, whether historical or rhetorical, has disappeared. The means of popular education, however, are still abundant ; for no village in India is without its schoolmaster, who enjoys a portion of tax-free land from the village, in virtue of his office. Nor is there the son of a Brahmin, or of a merchant, banker, or tradesman, throughout all India, who has not been taught to read and write with ease, if not with elegance : the former, in order to perform his duties as a teacher of religion, or as a clerk in a public office : the latter, to conduct his business as a book-keeper and accountant. It is true, that at present this is the extent of their education ; but what a mighty instrument is thus ready made to our hands, for conveying useful and general instruction through the village institutions, if the Government would, as it certainly might do, require that each village schoolmaster should in future undergo an examination, and obtain a certificate of qualification, before he was allowed to assume his office, whenever it devolved on him ; but such measures must be conducted *through the agency of the natives themselves.* If we look at the progress made in the arts and manufactures, before we came among them, we shall find they were little inferior to ourselves in almost all that is performed by manual labour. They were once deeply skilled in the sciences of astronomy, mathematics, and medicine; indeed, Dr. Royle (an author whose knowledge and experience is extensive, and whose authority is very high) is of opinion, that much that was known to the Greeks and to the Arabians, of pharmacy, was acquired from the Hindoos. It has been lately shown, that the people of the South of India alone possessed the secret of making steel in the time of Alexander the Great, and that they manufacture it at the present time on principles as scientific as any that have been adopted for the same purpose in Europe. (Cheers.) With regard to their knowledge of agriculture, I have myself witnessed it conducted (*on tax-free lands*) with as much skill as one sees here—aye, in Scotland—which is saying all that can be said for the art—(Hear, hear)—and in horticulture, as regards pruning, budding, grafting, and propagating by layers, they have nothing to learn from the West. It is of a people placed thus high in the scale of human knowledge, of whom I am now addressing you. (Hear, hear.) It is not for the savages of North America, the Negroes and Hottentots of Africa, nor the cannibals of the islands of the Pacific Ocean, that I ask your sympathy and claim your protection, though all these are justly entitled to those benevolent regards which I am happy to find you have bestowed on them. The people of whom I now speak, were in an advanced state of civilisation when our forefathers painted their bodies, and wore the skins of beasts. (Hear, hear.) It is the misfortunes brought on them by the natural effects of despotism and internal bad government, that have rendered them subject to foreign yokes during the last eight centuries. They have lost perhaps some of that high polish which literature imparts, and which belongs only to nations in a state of prosperity; but they have neither forgotten, nor have they lost, those venerable institutions which prevail, more or less, under their native princes, but which it is to be regretted that our ignorance, on the one hand, and the contempt in which we usually hold what we do not understand, on the other, have combined to disregard, to trample under foot, and to destroy. (Cheers.) Those institutions, of which Europeans in general know little, require only to be studied and comprehended, to form the ground-work of future good government; but, in our present state of information, we rule the country blindly and selfishly, and are the indirect, I might rather say the direct, cause of the dreadful calamities which, alas! too frequently visit it in the shape of dearth. I have said, Sir, our nation is ignorant of every thing regarding India, except some of the miseries which it occasionally endures; but it is owing to the exertions of such societies as this, that the people of this country are beginning to be informed. (Cheers.)

So much has been said lately on the subject of the famines that have desolated that beautiful land, that it will be unnecessary for me to dwell at large on them. I will, however, just glance at those which have occurred within the last twenty years of peace on the Indian continent, an event, it should be observed, without parallel in the course of our rule. In 1820-21, a famine raged in the southern part of the Deccan. In 1822-23, another famine prevailed over the same tract of country. In 1823-24, famine also prevailed from Caudeish in lat. 22, to Mysore in 14, an extent of nearly 500 miles. In 1833, a famine extended more to the eastward, over an area of 50,000 square miles; and during the months of March, April, and May, there were no fewer than eight thousand persons fed daily by the Government alone, in the city of Madras, besides those who shared the bounty of private establishments, formed for the purpose, all over the country, to which natives and Europeans alike contributed. In 1835-36, the famine spread over the northern portions of the Madras provinces, and extended to Orissa. In 1837-38, the greatest of all the famines prevailed in the north-western provinces of the Bengal presidencies, which carried off, as we are told, 500,000 human beings; and, strange to relate, during the latter period, as much grain was exported from the lower parts of Bengal as would have fed half a million of people at a pound of rice a day for a whole year! (Shame.) In the last and present year, dearth has made its appearance again, within the Bombay and Madras presidencies, and threatens a repetition of a similar calamity. Of such things we are at length fully informed; and shall we not ask, How that land, which once was a land flowing with milk and honey, and as capable as our own beloved country, of becoming like it the garden of the universe, has so fallen off? Why these famines occur so frequently, and why they are not averted? (Hear, hear.) Does the Government do nothing to ward off these evils? I answer, nothing. (Hear, hear.) When the evil arrives it does exert itself. It opens the public treasury—it establishes alms-houses—it employs those who can work, but how long can any country continue populous, or even inhabited at all, with such frightful desolation, so frequently repeated? (Hear, hear.) Or what government can afford to dole out of the public purse food to its famishing subjects with one hand, while it is compelled to remit its revenue on the other? (Hear.) All this, too, has happened at a period when its rulers have engaged in a war, and have adopted a policy, which, in the West, will advance the frontier of our Indian empire to the very frontiers of the Russian dominions, since Persia may now be deemed an integral part of them. While again, we are only awaiting the success of that expedition to commence another war in the East on the side of Burmah, which cost the Indian people, a few years ago, sixteen millions sterling, and which, from the position it left us in, involves the necessity of this new evil. It is not on a political question we are met to-night; and this subject should not have been introduced, but that such military expeditions do materially affect the means, when there may be the inclination to do good to the inhabitants, who are bound to pay the expense of such wars. It is in that point of view only, I say, such extravagant political projects do indirectly affect the bettering the condition of our fellow-subjects in the East. (Cheers.) But unhappily for them, the improvement of their condition is the last thing that is thought of; and yet, if one reads the accounts of the money that is annually expended on public works, one might fancy that much is done. In order to elucidate this, I will take the liberty of reading an extract from a Bombay newspaper, dated 18th May, 1839, the channel of the Government panegyric:—

" We have often endeavoured to prove that one of the greatest obstacles to Indian prosperity, is the wretched condition of the roads, and other means of communication. We have shown, in a former number, that, until the year 1830, we derived no agricultural produce whatever from the vast and fertile plains of Berar, and supplied that district with but a single article, viz., salt, which, owing to the almost impracticable condition of the roads, was conveyed from this place on the backs of bullocks, a distance of 600 miles. In that year, one of the native salt merchants tried the experiment of conveying back to Bombay, upon his returning bullocks, some of the cotton which abounds in that country; the experiment was completely successful, and next year, 10,000 loads were brought by the same means. In 1836, 90,000 loads were received from that one district. The road, however, if it can be so called, is still in such a condition, that the conveyance of the article to our market imposes an additional charge of 80 per cent. upon its original price ; a sum, we need scarcely say, literally lost to the seller, the buyer, and the country. The subject has at length been taken up by the Government. Surveys have been made, and a plan for the construction of a good wheel carriage road has been sent home for the sanction of the Court of Directors, the estimated expense being upwards of thirty thousand pounds. The extension of this line to Calcutta would, we may observe, not cost more than forty or fifty lacs, four or five hundred thousand pounds, and would be attended with unspeakable advantages to both sides of India.

" The necessity of something deserving the name of road, between Bombay and Agra, is now felt by every one, and the Governments of both Presidencies have zealously entered upon its construction. The distance between the two places is stated to be 782 miles. The road is actually completed for 277 miles, and surveys of the remaining portion are in progress. We shall, at an early period, notice this subject more fully. Besides these two great lines, other shorter ones, in various parts of the Bombay presidency, are, some actually begun, others in course of survey : and others again, after having received the sanction of the Indian Governments, are under reference to the authorities at home.

" Such are the promises of a better system which we remark throughout the provinces ;—the spirit of improvement is still more active at the Presidency. In proof of this assertion, we shall merely notice the various works, which, having met with the approval and sanction of Government, are at this moment under reference to the authorities at home.

" 1. A large additional yard for shipping to be made near the saluting battery, with slips, capable of building ships of war of the first class. Expense estimated at three lacs.

" 2. Lengthening the upper old dock for the admission of large steamers.

" 3. Erection of three slips for steamers, to the eastward of the present dock-yard.

" 4. Building extra coal-depots at Calaba, (estimate now in preparation.)

" 5. Building of new Court-house and offices; estimate, one lac and 69,000 rupees, (£16,900.)

" 6. Large public building, to include a Bank, Post-office, Exchange, and apartments for other public offices ; estimate, one lac.

" Besides these, there are just finished, or are about to be finished :—

" 7. An extensive sea-wall and quay, from Bhore-bunder to the Slaughter-house.

" 8. The beautiful new tower to the Cathedral, to be finished, we understand, next month.

" 9. The elegant Bazaar gates now completed."

Thus it is in every thing. When we ask what has the Government done for the direct benefit of the people in public works, there is exhibited, among others, a list of roads that have been made, and a few drains or ditches cut in the neighbourhood of the Presidencies, whose origin may be traced to the convenience of the European population. On referring to the Parliamentary returns, made by the East India Company, of public works executed in India, I find in the list a description of roads termed *military roads*, and of bridges denominated in Bengal *Shakspeare bridges*, so called after a gentleman who was once Postmaster-General, and who adopted a plan for transmitting the foot post over mountain torrents, which frequently impeded it during the rainy season. Then, of these military roads, there is hardly one of them over which I have not travelled ; and I say, without fear of contradiction, that there is scarcely ten miles of any part of them on which, during the rains, a carriage could be driven, or a loaded cart proceed without danger. (Hear, hear.) Roads are marked out, it is true, they are levelled for the time being, and, till the wet season sets in, they are tolerably good ; but one or two years serve to break them up entirely ; roads without metal, without drains, without bridges,—and, to be rendered available even for the march of an army with its stores, a detachment of pioneers is required to precede the troops. (Hear.) There is another description of roads, however, to which much attention and money is devoted. I mean the roads within and around the Presidencies, and the principal civil and military stations. Each road not extending beyond three or four miles in length, and used purely for European gentlemen and ladies to drive their carriages. (Hear, hear.) Another feature in the road-making of India must not be forgotten, and this is the practice of constructing roads to render places of retreat during the hot months conveniently accessible to governors, judges, and other Europeans, who are prompted to visit them on account of ill health or pleasure. I allude especially to those roads leading up to the salutary hill retreats of the Nilghirries from Madras, and the Mahableswur hills from Bombay. There, stupendous difficulties to the approach of hitherto inaccessible mountains, of 9000 feet in the one case, and half that height in the other, have been overcome for the purpose of conducting the European's palanquin with convenience suited to the luxuries of the East, to those hitherto unfrequented regions. (Hear.) The person who most devoted his attention to road-making in India, was your late honoured representative, Lord William Bentinck, than whom no one ever evinced a greater sympathy for our native population, or more desired to better their condition, provided always that it could be effected with economy. (Cheers.) It is to him the people owe the road of 227 miles in length, which is alluded to in the Bombay paper of the 18th May, an extract from which has been read. This road was finished in 1831, and it was then intended to carry it on to Omrawutty, in the heart of the cotton districts ; but eight years have elapsed without fulfilling the intention, and we now learn, as if for the first time, that an estimate has actually been submitted to England for sanction. (Hear.) Such has been the effect of making this road, that although only *four hundred* wheel carriages passed to and fro during the second year that it was opened, there were, in 1837-38, no fewer than *six thousand* carts plying on it ; but as the cotton has to be brought from Berar, the place of its growth, two hundred and fifty miles to the road, it is still dispatched on pack bullocks, and is so carried to its journey's end ; and the road is, as far as that traffic is concerned, at present useless. (Hear.) As an instance of the resources of the country, both in the materials and in the skill of the natives, it will not be amiss to mention, that an iron suspension bridge, of two hundred feet span, over which carriages pass, was constructed by the officer who superintended this very road, at the trifling cost of £4,800 sterling, under his supervision by the natives, without the aid of any European artificer. (Cheers.) Dr. Spry, in his work, entitled " Modern India," thus speaks of this bridge :—

" This suspension bridge has been constructed entirely out of the resources of the district, and by an amateur mechanic, who had never seen an iron suspension bridge in his life ! and yet we have an assurance from the visiting engineer for the north-western provinces and Central India, Major Irvine, C. B., that he had seen nothing superior to it in England. The undertaking was altogether an experimental one ; for, as I have elsewhere mentioned, there are no roads in this part of the country of any extent, and, consequently, little or no traffic between remote places ; its undertaking, therefore, originated in a desire to ascertain the capabilities of the materials and the workmen employed."

After a minute history of the progress and completion of the work, Dr. Spry says :—"Notwithstanding the countless extra expenses incidental to a first undertaking of this kind, and the distance to which all the materials were obliged to be transported, from the work-yard at Saugor to the place of erection, the bridge has been pronounced cheaper than those in Calcutta constructed of English materials. Here, then, we have a structure which, in elegance, in magnitude, and in durability, may vie with the most perfect specimens of the kind in civilized Europe; and yet, fashioned out of the oxydised metal as it lies embedded in the bowels of the earth, by the rude hands of a class of artizans, by no means as expert as their countrymen in Northern Hindostan ; and the whole emanating from the genius and unremitting industry of one master-mind! Does not this speak volumes? Does it not satisfactorily show what India can do when her resources are properly drawn forth? And is it not a reproof to all who would seek alike to depreciate the country and the capabilities of her people? While an empire possesses engineers and artificers, who are able to accomplish such a work as the Saugor Iron Suspension Bridge, the infusion of capital is all that is required to render that country great among the civilized kingdoms of the world; and to this point must India arrive, if proper steps be taken to bring her capabilities into active exertion." (Loud cheers.)

After this, what might not be effected by the ingenuity and industry of the natives themselves. (Cheers.) Roads, and bridges, and canals, are so essential to the prosperity of a country, that the first thing every settler in the back woods of America thinks of is, how he is to convey the produce of his farm to market, and how he is to obtain the articles he may himself require from the nearest town. Now, unfortunately, the people of India are kept by our defective system of finance so poor that they cannot themselves afford to make roads; and the Government itself has hitherto looked upon their construction as an object to be attempted only after prosperity has been obtained, rather than as one of the first steps to accomplish it. (Cheers.) And what, Sir, do you think the roads and canals, which have been constructed throughout so extensive a region, has cost the state within the last forty years? Why, less than was expended on the railway of thirty miles which connects Liverpool with Manchester. (Cheers.) Whenever a road is proposed by a public functionary, and recommended by the Government there to the Home authorities here —(the constituted Guardians and Protectors of India!)—they are told the finances do not admit of the expense ; but if government palaces are to be repaired or built—if court-houses are required for the convenience of European judges—or public offices for European collectors—or expensive barracks for European soldiers—or magazines for military stores—there are abundance of funds ; and if there are none, why, money is taken up in loans, so that the Indian public debt amounts, at this moment, to nearly forty millions of pounds sterling. (Hear, hear, and cheers.) Nothing, however, is ever borrowed or expended to improve the condition of the people of India, who alone pay the interest of such loans. (Hear.) When the Americans require to make roads they come to London and borrow the money, rather than be without them. They justly consider such debts to be like those a farmer contracts for a time to purchase seed—(cheers) —but the Indian Government, less wise, keeps in its treasury, in hard cash, from year's end to year's end, a sum of from eight to nine millions, about half the amount of the whole revenue, which lies idle and is withdrawn from currency, in a country where paper money is unknown, while it pays five per cent. on a debt of nearly forty millions contracted in making unprofitable wars. (Hear, hear.) If the Government would but put their specie into circulation instead of hoarding it up in their cash chest—if they would but expend the £400,000 or the £450,000 a-year they now pay in interest by this arrangement, in constructing useful public works for the benefit of the people, they would be sowing a fruitful crop which would yield to the State an abundant harvest. (Loud cheers.) I must now advert to another permanent, and, indeed, the most grievous calamity under which the afflicted people of India have been suffering, are suffering, and I fear are long likely to suffer, unless they be relieved by some novel and extraneous means, to which neither the Government here nor the natives of India have been accustomed,—exposure in regard to the former ; and sympathy and English advocacy in favour of the latter. The subject I allude to is THE LAND TAX OF INDIA. (Loud cries of hear, hear.) It is a subject which, owing to the ignorance of Europeans, has been involved in intricacy, and is environed (in the present state of information, and mode of thinking of our Indian legislators,) with difficulties which they consider insuperable, difficulties which arise out of a perverseness on their own parts ; originating partly in ignorance and partly in supineness. To explain this state of things, it would be necessary to enter into a detail of which the time does not admit, but it may be sufficient to say that the whole solves itself into these two questions—Are we, or are we not, proprietors or landlords of the soil in India? (hear, hear) and, if we are so, is it expedient that we should derive the full rent from our own lands ? To this I reply, and I challenge the Court of Directors—aye, and the whole world—to contradict me, that by right the Government is not the proprietor of the soil (loud cheers) ; that we have assumed to be true that which is absolutely false; and that the main secret of the cause of the distress of the people, and of the Government as to its finances, originates in that erroneous, unjust, and cruel assumption. (Cheers.) A right unclaimed by our predecessors, and unheard of in history. I repeat, Sir, unheard of in history. Who ever heard of a state proclaiming itself an universal landlord (hear)—the proprietor of every man's field, to take from it what suits it ? (Cheers.) Fields which have descended in India from father to son, and which have been tilled by the same family for generations ; or fields which have been bought and sold hundreds of times, during hundreds of years, without so monstrous a claim put forth on the part of Government ; but whenever any Government assumes a right to tax the soil to any amount that it chooses, then I admit that Government virtually becomes the owner, if it please, of the soil ; but only in the same way that a robber becomes the owner of my purse when he has compelled me to deliver it up to him. (Great cheering.) This is no hyperbole. It is no figure of speech. It is simply true. When the Indian or any other Government shall tax my house or my land, so as to compel me to abandon either one or the other, it may call itself proprietor, and exercise that privilege by might, which right, if respected, would prevent. (Hear, hear.) Neither the Hindoo nor the Mohammedan Sovereigns, though arbitrary enough in all conscience, ever perpetrated this injustice. They never claimed a proprietary right in every man's field, but they did claim as a tax a *limited* portion of the crop, a barbarous exaction to be sure, and calculated to depress industry, as the clerical tithe did till lately in England ; but still a certain portion, not less than three-fourths of the remainder of the crop, was left to the farmer. When the native Government desired to convert its portion into money, it had to look out a purchaser, and usually endeavoured to sell it to the cultivator himself; but in most instances it was sold through the small country banker, or grain merchant, who paid the cash into the treasury ; and, if required to advance the money, he received a bonus for the same, and made the best of his bargain. The British Government considered this practice objectionable on two accounts ; first, as becoming a partner in the labour and capital of the farmer ; and secondly, as being attended with all the inconvenience of converting the grain into rupees. So, without further ado, it fixed an assumed capability on every field to produce (hear) ; it fixed an assumed price on the produce itself (hear, hear) ; and it then fixed from thirty-five to forty-five per cent. of the money value of that produce as its share for ever ; excepting, indeed, when the proprietor should lay out money and dig a well, so as to irrigate his land, when a new assessment was made in proportion to the increased value of the crop. (Hear, hear, and cheers.) Now, as any person who ever cultivated a field in his life, or who ever sold its produce from year to year, knows that the same field does not yield the same quantity of corn every year, nor does corn fetch the same price in the market every year, so may he conceive what must be the condition of the landowner who has to make up, in money, to the Government at the end of every harvest, 45 per cent. of what his field was supposed to yield when corn is of only half the value that it was when the assessment was made. I hope I have made myself understood. (Cheers.) If I have, you will comprehend the condition of the Indian landholder, and the little chance there is, under the present system, of the millions of acres now lying waste ever being occupied to the benefit of the people, or to the advantage of the state. What is the result of this system? The land is abandoned by the owner. The Government makes a similar bargain with some one else who has no title to occupy the same land except that which an arbitrary Government gives after compelling the real owner to desert it ; and this new tenant, entering on his farm with a favourable condition for the first three or four years, abandons it also when the time for paying the full assessment arrives. If there be any one present who can look on this picture with apathy, I envy not his feelings. (Cheers.) The lands are taxed till they are driven out of cultivation—the roads are neglected, and the produce, if raised, in excess of the demands on the spot, is left to rot—the abundance of one district cannot be conveyed to prevent famine in another—little else but edible grains is cultivated for want of markets, the people are excluded from all share in the administration of their own concerns ; their institutions are neglected or overthrown ; their punchayat, or trial by jury, in civil or in criminal cases, is withheld from them, and they are handed over to the justice of a foreigner, generally ill acquainted with their language, unacquainted with their habits, and who has no sympathy for, nor feels the least interest in, the whole race to which the parties belong. There is no injustice in the fiscal and municipal administration which India has escaped ; nor in her commercial intercourse which she has not been made to endure. (Cheers.) Who is to blame? I answer, England, aye, all England! (Cheers) which transfers the destiny of a people and a country, little short in extent and population to Christian Europe, to the mercy of those few who are permitted to govern her, and who govern but with one view, the advantage of the mother country, to the ruin of India. (Hear, hear.) Who is it that refuses to listen to the appeals made from year to year, by the Governors on the spot, on the abuses of the land tax, but the Home authorities ? (Cheers.) Who is it that, in spite of justice, has imposed, and continues to impose, commercial laws, which compel India to receive, without duties, all the raw products of England, such as the metals, &c., and imposes from ten to twenty, nay, in some cases, one thousand per cent., on her raw produce when imported into England? (Hear.) Who is it that causes no higher a duty than two and a half per cent. on England's manufactured goods imported into India, to be levied, and lays from ten to twenty per cent. duty on some, and more than one hundred per cent. on others? The Parliament of Great Britain. (Loud cheers.) What other colony is treated in this way? Which of our colonies is wholly unrepresented, directly or indirectly, as is India? What protection has she against the grossest injustice, and to whom can she appeal with hope of redress? I reply, no where on earth. Her appeal is wafted in sighs, and is exhibited in tears at the throne of God. (Loud cheers.) Is this the way in which the people, whom we term free, should be treated? Is this the way in which those people, whom I have before described, deserve to be dealt with? What is the result of this absurd and even iniquitous conduct? Does India contribute a large revenue per head to the State? No. While England contributes £2, her colonies, aye, slave colonies, too, contributed from 30s. to 32s. 6d. per head; while the convict colonies of Van Diemen's Land pay £2 12s., and Sydney £3 a head in taxes, what does the Government receive from the poor Indian? not quite 4s.! While the same colonies, which I have described, consume £5 of our manufactures per head, India literally consumes but sixpenny worth. Reflect on these facts; consider what these people would contribute in revenue, and take of our manufactures, if ruled with wisdom I was going to say, but I say with common sense and common justice. Shall these people continue to be so misruled? Forbid it justice—forbid it heaven! I feel that all which is required to set these matters right, is to place them in their true light before my countrymen of Great Britain. I know they only want to be informed correctly, and they will demand justice. India will not continue without representatives! She will be represented in the British India Society. I feel confident there is no philanthropic heart in this building, that does not at this moment beat with indignation and with sympathy at the picture I have drawn, and I look to the time when thousands, nay hundreds of thousands, of generous Britons will, when the true state of that fair land shall be known, unite and make themselves heard, whenever it becomes necessary, through their own representatives in Parliament, and that they will finally obtain—JUSTICE FOR INDIA! (Protracted cheering.) I move the following Resolution:—

" That it is established, by ample evidence, that there exists throughout British India—a country of vast extent and great fertility, whose inhabitants are intelligent and industrious, and whose ancient institutions might be made instrumental to good government—an amount of destitution and misery, which demand the immediate sympathy and succour of the people of Great Britain."

Wm. Craig, Esq., seconded the Resolution.

The Chairman said, after the important facts laid before them, in a manner that breathed such a spirit of humanity and freedom, and at the same time in sentiments so noble, he was sure that they would carry the Resolution with one heart and soul. (Cheers.) The Resolution was then carried unanimously.

Mr George Thompson rose amidst loud cheers, and said,—Sir, I congratulate you and this great meeting upon the arrival of the first Anniversary of the day which witnessed the bestowal of entire freedom upon the coloured population of the West India Colonies. I congratulate you upon the admirable and irreproachable conduct of those upon whom this right was conferred by the justice of the British nation—they were unrevengeful while they were slaves, and they have been equally grateful and tractable as freemen. (Cheers.) Their conduct has been marked by prudence, firmness, reasonableness, and industry. (Cheers.) While they have not pliantly and submissively bent to the will of the planter, neither have they been unmindful of the interests and righteous claims of those above them. (Loud and continued cheering.) I congratulate you upon the freedom granted to the apprenticed bondsmen of Mauritius, on the 31st of March last. I congratulate you upon the progress of the cause of human rights in the United States, as depicted in the burning words of my unflinching and well-beloved friend, WILLIAM LLOYD GARRISON. (Cheers.) Finally, I congratulate you upon the prospect of a convention of the friends of the Slave from different parts of the world, to be held during the ensuing year, to consider the plans which remain to be adopted for the entire and universal overthrow of Slavery and the Slave Trade. (Loud cheers.)

And now, permit me to leave the language of congratulation, and, by an abrupt transition, to strike.for a moment a mournful chord. I cannot resist a spontaneous impulse to embrace this, the first public opportunity, of expressing my deep sympathy with those around me, in the loss which this Society, this city, and the general interests of humanity have sustained, in the removal, by the hand of death, of one whom I loved as a friend, admired as a citizen, and venerated as a man of God,—one who was among the earliest, the warmest, and the steadiest friends of this Society. Need I pronounce the name of PATRICK LETHEM? We cherish his memory, we hallow his dust: may we catch his glorious spirit, and follow out his noble purposes!

I shall take the liberty, Sir, of adding, what I think will be deemed valuable, to the information already given respecting the state of the Anti-Slavery cause in the United States. It has been my privilege to receive, very recently, a number of letters from distinguished Abolitionists in America, and having several of their communications with me at present, I shall lay an extract or two before this meeting. My friend, J. G. WHITTIER, the well-known Quaker bard of America, thus writes:— "The struggle still goes on. Discussion, every where—in the churches, the parlour, the workshop, the stage, the steam-boat, and the rail-road car." [I heard this evening some honest friend exclaim, " We have white slaves at home." If such there be, behold the way to set them free! Let there be no unlawful outbreaks; but calm, rational, open discussion —discussion every where. The grievances will then soon become apparent; the remedy too, and the ends of justice will be obtained.] My friend continues—" Discussion goes on in the State Legislatures, and in the Halls of Congress. Discussion literally shakes the nation. We are struggling apparently against fearful odds—but our confidence is strong. The strength of God is pledged on the side of humanity. Some of us, who have been striving from the outset, occasionally grow weary—the harness of our warfare, worn day and night, sometimes galls with its links of iron, and we long for peace and quiet, but the cry of our brother in bonds is in our ear, and we cannot yield to this weakness of the flesh. We must fight on." My next extract is from the pen of H. B. STANTON, Corresponding Secretary of the American Anti-Slavery Society. He says:—" The great cause is *onward* in the United States. Our Committee will make unprecedented exertions during the present year, to press our principles on the public consideration. We are to hold a National Anti-Slavery Convention on the 31st of July. On the 1st of August we shall celebrate the glorious Anniversary of West India Emancipation." (Cheers.)

I have now great pleasure in laying before this meeting a letter from a highly respected and noble-minded American citizen, now in this country —WENDEL PHILLIPS, Esq., of Boston. This accomplished scholar and warm-hearted Abolitionist, who has for a time relinquished the pursuit of an honourable profession, that he may devote himself to the cause of his enslaved countrymen, has done me the honour to address to me the letter which I hold in my hand, and which I shall submit entire, as a document well entitled to your consideration, not less on account of the importance of the topics which it discusses, than for the elegance and force of the language which it employs. I am particularly struck with the just and statesmanlike views which Mr PHILLIPS has adopted, in reference to the recent attempt to bring the subject of India before this country, by means of a British India Society. This letter will bring me, by a natural process, to the subject upon which I am particularly anxious to address you to-night, and upon which I shall dwell for a few moments, if you do not see cause to dismiss me. (Cheers.) The following is the letter :—

" LONDON, *July* 29*th*, 1839.

" MY DEAR THOMPSON,—I am very sorry to say *No* to your pressing request, but I cannot come to Glasgow, duty takes me elsewhere ; my heart will be with you though, on the 1st of August ; and I need not say how much pleasure it would give me to meet, on that day especially, the men to whom my country owes so much, and on the spot dear to every American Abolitionist, as the scene of your triumphant refutation and stern rebuke of Breckenridge. I do not think any of you can conceive the feelings with which an American treads such scenes. You cannot realize the debt of gratitude he feels to be due, and is eager to pay, to those who have spoken in behalf of humanity, and whose voices have come to him across the water. The Vale of Leven, Exeter Hall, Glasgow, and Birmingham, are consecrated spots—the land of Scoble and Sturge, of Wardlaw and Buxton, of Clarkson and O'Connell, is ' hallowed ground' to us. Would I could be with you, to thank the English Abolitionists, in the Slave's name, for the great experiment they have tried in behalf of humanity—for proving, in the face of the world, the safety and expediency of Immediate Emancipation—for writing out the demonstration of the problem, as if with letters of light on the blue vault of heaven—to thank them, too, for the fidelity with which they have rebuked the apathy, and denounced the guilt of the American Church, in standing aloof from this great struggle for freedom, in modern times. The appeals and exhortations which have from time to time gone out from among you, may seem to have fallen to the ground in vain ; but far from it : they have awakened, in some degree at least, a slumbering Church to a great national sin, and they have strengthened greatly, hands which were almost ready to faint in the struggle with a giant evil. We need them still—spare us not a moment from your Christian rebukes—give us line upon line, and precept upon precept. Our enterprise is eminently a religious one, dependent for success entirely on the religious sentiment of the people. It is on hearts that wait not for the results of West India experiments—that look to duty, and not to consequences—that disdain to make the *fears* of one class of men the *measure* of the rights of another—that dread no evil in the doing of God's commands—it is on such that the weight of our cause mainly rests, and on the conversion of those, whose characters will make them such, that its future progress must depend. It is upon just such minds that your appeals have most effect. I hardly exaggerate when I say, that the sympathy and brotherly appeals of British Christians are the sheet-anchor of our cause. Did they realise, that Slavery is most frequently defended now in America from the Bible—that when Abolitionists rebuke the Church for upholding it, they are charged with hostility to Christianity itself, they would feel this. If we construe a text in favour of liberty, it is set down to partiality and prejudice. A *European* construction is decisive. *Our* rebukes lose much of their force, when they are represented, though falsely, to spring from personal hostility—from a zeal which undue attention to a single subject has made to outrun discretion. *Your* appeals sink deep—they can neither be avoided nor blunted by any such pretence, and their first result must be conviction. Distance lends them something of the awful weight of the verdict of posterity. May they never cease. Let the light of your example shine constantly upon us, till our Church, beneath its rays, like Egypt's statue, shall break forth into the music of consistent action.

"England, too, is the fountain head of our literature. The slightest censure, every argument, every rebuke on the pages of your Reviews, strikes on the ear of the remotest dweller in our country. Thank God that in this the sceptre has not yet departed from Judah—that it dwells still in the land of Vane and Milton, of Pym and Hampden, of Sharp, and Cowper, and Wilberforce—

'The dead, but sceptred sovereigns,
Who still rule our spirits from their urns.'

May those upon whom rests their mantle be true to the realms they sway. You have influence where we are not even heard. The prejudice which treads under foot the vulgar Abolitionist dares not proscribe the literature of the world. In the name of the Slave, I beseech you let that literature speak out in deep, stern, and indignant tones ; for the press,

'Like the air,
Is seldom heard but when it speaks in thunder.'

"I am rejoiced to hear of your new movement in regard to India. It seals the fate of the Slave System in America. The industry of the Pagan shall yet wring from Christian hands the prey they would not yield to the commands of conscience, or the claims of religion. (Cheers.) Hasten the day ! for it lies with you, when the prophecy of our Randolph, (himself a Slaveholder) shall be fulfilled—that the time would come when masters would fly their Slaves, instead of Slaves their masters, so valueless would be a Slave's labour in comparison with his support. To you—to the sunny plains of Hindostan we shall owe—that our beautiful prairies are unpolluted by the footstep of a Slaveholder—that the march of civilization westward will be changed from the progress of the manacled Slave coffle, at the bidding of the lash, to the quiet step of families carrying peace, intelligence, and religion, as their household gods. (Loud cheers.) Mr Clay has cooly calculated the value of sinews and muscles—of the bodies and souls of men—and then asked us whether we could reasonably expect the south to surrender 1,200,000,000 of dollars at the bidding of abstract principles ? Be just to India,—waken that industry along her coast, which oppression has kept landlocked and idle—break the spell which binds the genius of her fertile plains, and we shall see this property in man become like the gold in India's fairy tales—dust in the Slaveholder's grasp. (Applause.) You cannot imagine, my dear brother, the impulse this new development of England's power will give the Anti-

Slavery cause in America. (Hear, hear.) It is just what we need to touch a class of men who seem almost out of the pale of religious influence. Much as our efforts have been blessed ;—much as they have accomplished,—though truth has often floated further on the shouts of a mob, than our feeble voices could have carried it,—still, our progress has served but to show us more clearly the Alps which lie beyond. The evil is so deep-rooted, the weight of interest and prejudice enlisted on its side so vast—ambition clinging to political power, wealth to the means of further gain—that we have sometimes feared they would be able to put off Emancipation till the charter of the Slaves' freedom would be sealed with blood —that our day of freedom would be like Egypt's, when " God came forth from his place, His right hand clothed in thunder," and the jubilee of Israel was echoed by Egypt's wailing for her first-born. It is not the thoughtful, the sober-minded, the conscientious, for whom we fear. With them truth will finally prevail. It is not that we want eloquence or Christian zeal enough to sustain the conflict with such—and with your aid to come off conquerors. We know, as your Whately says of Galileo, that if Garrison could have been answered, he had never been mobbed— (Loud cheers)—that May's Christian firmness—Smith's world-wide philanthropy—Chapman's daring energy—and Weld's soul of fire—can never be quelled, and will finally kindle a public feeling, before which opposition must melt away. (Cheers.) But how hard to reach the callous heart of selfishness—the blinded conscience, over which a corrupt Church has thrown its shield, lest any ray of truth pierce its dark chambers ! How shall we address that large class of men with whom dollars are always a weightier consideration than duties—prices current stronger arguments than proofs of holy writ ? But India can speak in tones which will command a hearing. (Hear, hear.) Our appeal has hitherto been entreaty— for the times in America are those ' parsy times,' when

> ' Virtue itself of Vice must pardon beg—
> Yea, curb and woo, for leave to do him good.'

But, from India, a voice comes clothed with the omnipotence of self-interest, and the wisdom which might have been slighted from the pulpit, will be to such men, oracular from the market-place. (Cheers.) Gladly will we make a pilgrimage, and bow with more than eastern devotion on the banks of the Ganges, if his holy waters shall be able to wear away the fetters of the Slave. (Cheers.) God speed the progress of your Society ! May it soon find in its ranks the whole phalanx of sacred and veteran Abolitionists ! No single, divided effort, but a united one to grapple with the wealth, influence, and power, embattled against you. Is it not Schiller who says :—' Divide the thunder into single notes, and it becomes a lullaby for children—but pour it forth in one quick peal, and the royal sound shall shake the heavens ;' so may it be with you—and God grant, that without waiting for the ' United States to be consistent'— before our ears are dust, the jubilee of emancipated millions may reach us from Mexico to the Potomac, and from the Atlantic to the Rocky Mountains !—Yours truly, and most affectionately,

" WENDELL PHILLIPS."

(Loud cheers followed the reading of this letter.)

Sir, if I should now sit down, no one here would venture to say I had not made a very eloquent speech. (Cheers.) I said the letter of Mr Phillips would bring me naturally to the subject of *India* : you perceive it has done so. Mr Phillips attaches great, but not undeserved importance, to the question which, during the last twelve months, I have more than once had the honour of bringing before you. You are told that the successful prosecution of certain plans to raise and regenerate India, seals the fate of the Slave System of America. This is just—this is true. But do these projects respecting India admit of success—are they such as recommend themselves to reasonable and practical men? They are,—First, we point to the continents and islands of America. We say, see there, nearly six millions of human beings in Slavery, under a torturing lash and a vertical sun. Look next to Africa—hourly rent by wars, and plundered of her children.—Look at the irrefragable figures of Mr Buxton, which have demonstrated the soul-harrowing truth, that a thousand human beings are, during every four-and-twenty hours, butchered with steel, or bartered for gold, that the Slave Systems of Christian countries may continue. (Hear.) You ask, why this bloody and inhuman sacrifice of helpless beings—why this infernal machinery of whips and chains, and stocks and collars? I answer, that you may clothe yourselves in cotton—that you may drink coffee, and sweeten your draught with sugar—that you may dine on rice, or regale yourselves with tobacco. (Cheers.) Sir, were a man to drop from the clouds, and to be told these things, he would naturally infer that these articles were indispensable—that they could be grown only in America—that they could be produced only by Slave labour—that from Africa alone could Slaves be procured, and that they could only be kept at work by the inhuman means now employed. (Cheers.) What would he think—what would he say, if he were told that all these articles might be raised in the country from which the Slaves had been dragged—that an honourable and extensive commerce might be carried on without the necessity of wars, and without the horrors of Slavery? (Cheers.) What would he think, if told, that the people who are the chief consumers, and, therefore, the principal supporters of American Slavery, have an empire of their own—whose beauty cannot be exaggerated—whose extent is limitless —whose soil is exhaustlessly rich, and whose population is reckoned by scores of millions—from which they might obtain, without coercion, unbedewed with tears, unstained by blood, all that the wants and luxurious appetites of European—aye, and American nations, could possibly require. (Loud cheering.) What, I ask, would be the opinion of a visitant from another sphere, if told these things? (Hear, hear.) How do these things come to pass? Do the Americans, Brazilians, and French and Spanish colonists, instinctively delight in inflicting tortures? Is the love of chains and Slavery their ruling passion? No. They love money—they see that we are an enterprising, ingenious, and fabricating nation—that here is a market for their produce—that we ask no questions when we buy—that the price we give will support them in administering a system of forced labour, and they therefore adopt and follow the trade of planters in cotton and brokers in blood. (Cheers.) Scourges and fetters, bolts and thumbscrews, men-stealers and drivers, are but the instruments they use to accomplish a grand end, which is the reaping of gain by the supply of our unceasing demands. (Cheers.) And yet we are an Anti-Slavery nation —(Ironical cheers)—and yet we paid twenty millions to get rid of the abomination of Negro bondage in our own colonies—(Cheers)—and yet we have societies for the conversion of other nations to Abolition principles! Is there no inconsistency here? Are not our professions justly liable to reproach, and to be branded as insincere and hypocritical? While we are assembled here, to point our appeals across the Atlantic, that they may reach, if possible, the conscience of the American, might not a voice of thunder speak from every warehouse in this city, gorged with the produce of the Slave—from every spinning jenny and loom employed in the service of Slavery—" Woe unto you, Scribes, Pharisees, Hypocrites, for you send memorials, and missionaries, and remonstrances, over sea and land, to denounce the crime of holding men in bondage, while you yourselves stay at home to raise the wages of unrighteousness — the price of blood — and feed to fatness the cupidity of those who are willing to sell themselves to you in the service of sin." All this we should deserve if India were not ours—or if the country were blotted from the map of the world. How much more, while India is in existence—while India is an integral portion of our own dominions ? Why prefer New Orleans to Calcutta—Mobile to Bombay—Cuba to Madras? Why leave freemen famishing by millions on the banks of the Ganges and the Jumna, that you may steal men from the banks of the Gambia and the St. Mary's, and lash them to their hated task on the banks of the Mississippi and the Potomac ? (Great cheering.) But enough ; you see, you feel the crime of despising that splendid country and that interesting race, on whose behalf so eloquent an appeal has been made, in the honest, fearless, admirable speech, of my gallant friend MAJOR-GENERAL BRIGGS. (Cheers.) You are not called upon to cease your remonstrances against Slavery ; you are not required to forego any of the comforts or luxuries of life, or to circumscribe your trading operations, or to go to war with piratical nations, or to levy discriminating duties, or to enforce forgotten treaties ; or to call together Congresses of nations ; but quietly, consistently, but energetically, to improve your own territory—to employ your own husbandmen—to reap your own soil—in a word, to put into operation a principle of political economy, which would as surely work the destruction of Slavery and the Slave Trade, as the produce of the labour of fifty millions of freemen, procured at the rate of twopence per day for each man, must drive out of every market, where fair competition is permitted, the produce of six millions of Slaves, whose support averages from eighteen to thirty pence per day. (Cheers.) How truly unexceptionable, how simple, how patriotic, how certain, is the course thus pointed out! Let me, Sir, specify, in the fewest possible words, the principal grounds on which I deem it the duty of this nation, and of such a meeting as this, in particular, to take up the cause of India. India, in itself considered, is worthy of our regards. It is the largest, richest, and most available portion of our territory. The people, eighty or a hundred millions in number, are civilized, ingenious, docile, acute, and industrious—they are, besides, in need of our interposition to save them from an oppressive system, which is breeding discontent, and occasioning disease, and famine, and death. Their intellectual condition requires our consideration and aid. Various kinds of Slavery exist, which have to be inquired into and abolished, if within the legitimate sphere of our authority in that country. (Hear, hear.) The inhabitants of India, if raised from their present state of poverty, would become the best and largest consumers of the surplus manufactures of our own country. The political condition of India must be affected beneficially by every philanthropic effort, inasmuch as our tenure of dominion is the attachment of the people to our sway. Look then at India by itself. Half a million of square miles of territory ! Ought not its resources to be explored ? One hundred millions of inhabitants ! Ought not their wants to be considered ? They are poor, they must be fed— they are naked, they must be clothed—they are disaffected, they must be conciliated—they are industrious, they must be employed. Our humanity, our patriotism, our justice, are appealed to in behalf of British India. But my next ground is the Anti-Slavery aspect of the question. I see the battle of freedom for the degraded Slave transferred to the plains of India. (Cheers.) I see that we are every moment guilty of great inconsistency, if not crime, while we neglect India, and support the Slave Systems of America. I see that, in the circumstances of India, we have inexhaustible materials for Anti-Slavery appeals to this country ;—appeals to every class of motives by which men are moved to pity or impelled to action. I see that we possess, as a nation, the power of immediately diminishing, and ultimately destroying the Slave Trade and Slavery, by improving the condition of the natives, and developing the physical resources of India. (Cheers.) I see that we are placed in circumstances of fearful responsibility, and that we cannot justify our profession before men, nor clear our consciences before God, unless we use the means that are placed in our hands. I see, finally, that by calling attention to India, and exhibiting our pacific, yet powerful principles of action, we secure the attention and support of thoughtful, practical, and reasoning men—men who would turn from us if we professed to rely solely upon moral machinery against Slavery, *while our capital and trade were sustaining it*, but are ready to join us when our precepts and practice correspond, and the truth of our doctrines is recommended by the performance of our duties. I have no time to dwell, as I intended, upon the openings for commerce, and the acquisition of wealth which India presents—nor to trace, which I might have done most clearly, the extraordinary progress which has been made in the growth and exportation of every article which has received the least encouragement—such as indigo, linseed, &c. The elucidation of these and other topics must be deferred to another opportunity. I must, however, go back to the points mentioned by our distinguished visitor, General Briggs. It must not be disguised that there is a great work to be done before India can reward the industry, or obtain the benefit of the capital and enterprise of this country, and it is to this work that I want you and the country at large to gird yourselves. I remember the admonition given me by a friend to-day, who said,—" Pray, do not deal in the stale, vague talk about 'good government,' which means any thing or nothing, as folks please to interpret it, but tell us what India wants, and how we are to get it." I say then, that the Government of India, which shall deserve the name of *good*, will reduce and for ever fix the land-tax, which is now the curse of the country—blighting its produce—spreading sterility over the soil, and reducing the cultivator to the state of a beggar. When India is blessed with good government, her ancient institutions will be respected, her municipal machinery will be employed, her native teachers will be sent to their original and appropriate occupation, her rivers will be rendered navigable, roads and connecting canals will be made, and the produce of the lands will be admitted to these ports upon the principle of reciprocal duties. You will ask—how are these things to be obtained ? I answer, by agitation, by discussion, by petition. India, it is true, has a Board of Control, but India wants another Board. The Board of Control she wants is a Board consisting of the whole British people—alive to the claims of misery—awake to their own interests—sensible of their responsibility, and determined to do their duty. (Loud cheers.) Let these things be brought to pass, and the spell which has bound India shall be broken—a voice shall be heard crying from the banks of the Indus and the Ganges to the myriad population of our Eastern empire, " Arise, shine, for your light is come!"—the Hindoo shall raise his head and smile—the earth shall yield her increase—the riches of the East, not " barbaric gold and pearl" alone, but the bountiful crop of the industrious cultivator, shall find their way to these islands, and all who have laboured to succour and illuminate

India, shall rejoice in the reflex influence of their own benevolence. Sir, I will conclude. I rejoice in the prospects which are opening for India. I triumph by anticipation in the results which will, through India, be wrought out for the rest of the world. I call upon the Slave in America and the children of Africa to rejoice—but especially do I call upon my country to awake to a sense of her dread accountableness to God, for the use of the mighty power by which she can control the fortunes and the fate of so large a proportion of the whole human race. (Loud cheers.) To her I say,

> Britain! thy voice can bid the dawn ascend,
> On thee alone the eyes of Asia bend.
> High Arbitress! to thee her hopes are given,
> Sole pledge of bliss, and delegate of Heaven;
> In thy dread mantle all her fates repose,
> Or big with blessings, or o'ercast with woes;
> And future ages shall thy mandate keep,
> Smile at thy touch or at thy bidding weep.
> Oh! to thy god-like destiny arise!
> Awake and meet the purpose of the skies!
> Wide as thy sceptre waves let India learn,
> What virtues round the shrine of empire burn.

Mr Thompson moved the following Resolution, and sat down amid long-continued cheering:—

"That, considering the value of our Empire in India—the destitute and helpless condition of the many Millions of our Fellow-Subjects in that Country, and the intimate connexion between their Improvement and Prosperity as an Agricultural Population, and the Abolition of Slavery and the Slave Trade—this meeting regards with the purest satisfaction the formation, in London, of the BRITISH INDIA SOCIETY, and pledges itself to assist in promoting the great object which that Society has in view."

J. S. BLYTH, Esq., seconded the Resolution, which was carried with unanimous approbation.

THOMAS GRAHAME, Esq., proposed the last Resolution, viz.:—"Thanks to the Office-Bearers of both Societies—to the Ladies, for their valuable co-operation—to the Trustees, for the use of the Chapel; and to Dr. Wardlaw, for his conduct as Chairman"—which was carried with acclamations.

The meeting then broke up. The Chapel was crowded in every part, and, notwithstanding the length of the proceedings, the great mass of the people remained patiently till the end.

AMERICAN SLAVERY AS IT IS:

TESTIMONY OF

A THOUSAND WITNESSES!

No. II.

THE American Anti-Slavery Society has lately published, under the above title, says the *British Emancipator,* "a thick pamphlet of two hundred and twenty-four pages, closely printed in double columns, (containing therefore much more matter than many a portly octavo volume,) pourtraying, on indisputable authority, the actual condition of the Slaves, and the prevailing conduct of the Slaveholders, in the United States. It has been called for, not only by the want of specific and authentic information among those to whom American Abolitionists make their appeal for support, but by the incessant and vociferous boastings of Slaveholders themselves. , Being the only parties to do so, they are eminently unscrupulous in sounding their own praise. Hence the occasion of the work before us, and most powerfully is it adapted to its end. An extract from the introduction will clearly explain the scope of it.

" As Slaveholders and their apologists are volunteer witnesses in their own cause, and are flooding the world with testimony that their Slaves are kindly treated; that they are well fed, well clothed, well housed, well lodged, moderately worked, and bountifully provided with all things needful for their comfort, we propose, first, to disprove their assertions by the testimony of a multitude of impartial witnesses, and then to put Slaveholders themselves through a course of cross-questioning, which shall draw their condemnation out of their own mouths. We will prove that the Slaves in the United States are treated with barbarous inhumanity ; that they are overworked, underfed, wretchedly clad and lodged, and have insufficient sleep ; that they are often made to wear round their necks iron collars armed with prongs, to drag heavy chains and weights at their feet while working in the field, and to wear yokes, and bells, and iron horns ; that they are often kept confined in the stocks day and night for weeks together, made to wear gags in their mouths for hours or days, have some of their front teeth torn out or broken off, that they may be easily detected when they run away; that they are frequently flogged with terrible severity, have red pepper rubbed into their lacerated flesh, and hot brine, spirits of turpentine, &c., poured over the gashes to increase the torture ; that they are often stripped naked, their backs and limbs cut with knives, bruised and mangled by scores and hundreds of blows with the paddle, and terribly torn by the claws of cats, drawn over them by their tormentors; that they are often hunted with blood-hounds, and shot down like beasts, or torn in pieces by dogs; that they are often suspended by the arms, and whipped and beaten till they faint, and when revived by restoratives, beaten again till they faint, and sometimes till they die; that their ears are often cut off, their eyes knocked out, their bones broken, their flesh branded with red hot irons; that they are maimed, mutilated, and burned to death over slow fires. All these things, and more and worse, we shall *prove.* Reader, we know whereof we affirm, we have weighed it well ; *more and worse* WE WILL PROVE. Mark these words, and read on ; we will establish all these facts by the testimony of scores and hundreds of eye-witnesses, by the testimony of *Slaveholders* in all parts of the Slave States, by Slaveholding Members of Congress and of State Legislatures, by ambassadors to foreign courts, by judges, by doctors of divinity, and clergymen of all denominations, by merchants, mechanics, lawyers, and physicians, by presidents and professors in colleges and *professional* seminaries, by planters, overseers, and drivers. We shall show, not merely that such deeds are committed, but that they are frequent ; not done in corners, but before the sun; not in one of the Slave States, but in all of them ; not perpetrated by brutal overseers and drivers merely, but by magistrates, by legislators, by professors of religion, by preachers of the gospel, by Governors of States, by 'gentlemen of property and standing,' and by delicate females moving in the 'highest circles of society.'"— *Introduction,* p. 9.

" The promise here made is amply fulfilled both in letter and spirit.

" The Southerners, of course, are mad enough" at the galling exposures contained in this work; "but *disproof* is the thing required, and this is out of the question. Alas! poor Republicanism! O land so boastful of liberty and the rights of man, thine own sons have justly named thee ' SCORN OF THE NATIONS!' "

ASSEMBLIES, CONFERENCES, CONVENTIONS.

(*From the* NEW YORK EMANCIPATOR.)

" WE said, two numbers since, that 'among the most formidable enemies of the Slave, must be reckoned at present, the General Assemblies, General Conferences, and General Conventions of Christian churches.' We meant all we said.

" These bodies, it is understood, represent the best piety and intelligence of the several churches. The General Conference of the Methodists, particularly, is composed exclusively of preachers, who are presumed in general to have a more just appreciation of Christian truth, and to feel a deeper interest in its success, than the laity.

" Their great object is, the preservation and extension of sound doctrine and pure morals; all moral and religious subjects come legitimately under their notice. Whenever a heresy starts up that threatens the integrity of the church, it is their business to sound the alarm, and testify against it. Whenever a particular sin, lifting its head above the rest, endangers the purity of the church, they feel it to be their duty to point it out to special reprobation, and show its utter hostility to right principle. In a word, they are called upon to guard the health and purity of the church, set their faces against all error and sin, and especially to act not only against those heresies or sins which, under the circumstances, threaten the most serious encroachments on the kingdom of Christ; but also in favour of those institutions or practices, which, from existing causes, may be peculiarly necessary for the promotion of some vital interest.

" So well is this understood, that no one is surprised when these bodies pass solemn resolutions, denouncing lotteries, gambling, intemperance, and sabbath-breaking, and recommending sabbath-schools, temperance societies, &c. The duty of such action is manifest to all.

" Suppose one-third of the members of the Presbyterian church were addicted to the practice of sabbath-breaking. Many of their brethren, scandalized at such conduct, memorialize the General Assembly on the subject, earnestly praying it to pass resolutions, setting forth the duty of observing the sabbath-day, and condemning its violation as sin against God. Year after year similar memorials go up, but the Assembly, in some cases, will not act upon them; in others, is shaken to its centre by excited debates as to the propriety of considering them; and in every instance, steadily refuses to express any opinion with regard to their object. We ask what would be the effect, the necessary effect, of such conduct? Plainly, *to secure the sanction and support of the whole church to the practice of sabbath-breaking*. Thus the Assembly would be doing every thing in its power to destroy the obligation of sabbath observances, short of an Act expressly affirming the non-existence of such obligation.

" We have given a supposed case; we advert now to a real one.

" Slavery has taken up its abode in the American churches. It finds a welcome home in the southern portions of nearly all the large denominations. In the church, as in the state, different opinions concerning it are expressed. Some call it an evil; some, a great moral evil; some, a sin; some, one of the vilest sins under the sun: others will have it a Bible institution. Whatever it be, it has rapidly extended itself in form and spirit, and is now exciting discussion every where. It is emphatically the question of the age and country, and since the church is so deeply involved in the practice of Slaveholding, it is time its constituted authorities should give their opinion upon it.

" Memorials, praying that it may be recognized as a sin, and some action be taken against it, have of late years been repeatedly sent up to the bodies alluded to, but they have steadily refused to answer the prayers of the memorialists. Sometimes the memorials have been treated contemptuously, sometimes they have been acted on just far enough to show that, whatever might be the opinions of free State members, they have suffered themselves to be subjugated by southern dictation. In no instance, have these bodies, representing the piety and intelligence of the church, been induced to say that Slavery was wrong.

" As before in the case of sabbath-breaking, so now in this instance, we ask, what must be the effect of such conduct? Clearly, *to secure the sanction and support of the moral power of the church, to the practice of Slaveholding*. Is it not, then, true, that these bodies, whose decisions, whether expressed or implied, upon moral and religious subjects, must have weight proportioned to the amount of integrity and information which men concede to them, are among the most formidable enemies of human liberty?

" To be more particular, the evils which flow from such recreant conduct are these:—

" 1. With a certain class of persons, the character of ministers of the gospel for fidelity to their principles is greatly depreciated, and their influence curtailed.

"2. In the estimation of another class, Christianity itself is made to suffer detriment ; for if those who are fairly presumed to enjoy most of its light and favour, can thus find nothing in so unnatural a crime as Slavery to deserve their reprobation, surely the religion they preach is a worthless one. Absurd as such reasoning is, still that there are many who do thus reason, and by the immoral time-serving of Christian professors are taught to despise Christianity, is a well known fact.

"3. But a large majority are influenced in a different way. Retaining their confidence in these bodies, and their hold on Christianity, they learn gradually to look upon Slavery as a kind of misfortune, which, though not exactly right, God somehow or other tolerates, and therefore, had better be let alone. Thus, the Slaveholder is encouraged, the public conscience quieted, sympathy for the Slave abated, and the few who still struggle to bring about the year of jubilee, are pressed down by additional odium, and find new obstacles thrown in their way.

" For the blood of the poor, suffering captive, God will hold these religious bodies largely accountable."—*Philanthropist*.

BRETHREN, ARE THESE THINGS SO ?

" It is said and reiterated every day that the north is in no way responsible for the continuance of Slavery at the south: and that the churches at the north are not exerting any influence to uphold the system. The reader will see in the following article how, in one mode, *Northern Baptists* are keeping the Slaveholders in countenance. We have no doubt of the correctness of Brother Colver's statement; and do consider 'the pledge' in good keeping with one given by I. M. Allen, at that time Agent of the Baptist General Tract Society, some years ago, and with the general policy of many who exert some influence in the denomination. How long Baptists will be kept *mute* by such policy we know not. Let the facts be known.—Mr Allen is now the General Agent of the Baptist Bible Society. Let us have our minds, brethren, from every quarter of the land, on the propriety of the course pursued by the Board and Agent."—*Editor Reflector*.

" The Shaftsbury Association held its 59th Anniversary with the first Baptist Church in Shaftsbury, on the 5th and 6th inst. It was a good and profitable session. Most of the churches have enjoyed the quickening influences of the Spirit during the year. About 150, in the whole, have been added by baptism. Resolutions were adopted in support of the various benevolent operations of the day—among others, strong ones against Slavery. In regard to the *American and Foreign Bible Society*, Brother Nathaniel Colver introduced the following preamble and Resolution, which after remarks from Brother Colver and others, were adopted by a strong vote, no one dissenting:—

" Whereas we have learned, through the southern Baptist press, that a pledge has been given to the Slaveholders of the south, by the General Agent of the American and Foreign Bible Society, that the Society shall never in any way interfere with the institution of Slavery; and whereas said avowal has not been contradicted by the Agent, nor condemned by the Board; and whereas such pledge is a violation of the constitution of the Society—inasmuch as that declares the field to be the world—while such pledge makes an exception of [near] 3,000,000 of brethren in bondage, by pledging the Society to their oppressors beforehand, that we will not interfere with their unholy usurpations by giving to their victims the word of life—therefore,

" *Resolved,* That we have learned the above with great grief, and we do affectionately, as we desire the purity and harmony of our holy enterprise, entreat the Board to take early measures to cancel and repudiate such pledge.' "

" Brother Colver, in the course of his remarks supporting the Resolution, stated that the church in Greenwich, N.Y., raised a sum of money (100 dollars, I think,) for the Society, and forwarded it by him when he went to New York to attend the Anniversaries in May, instructing him to ascertain, if possible, whether the facts stated in the above preamble were founded in truth; if they were, to withhold the money and return it to the church, unless the Pro-Slavery act could be undone. Brother Colver, on inquiry and investigation had, was satisfied that the pledge had been given to the Slaveholders, and being unable to procure reaction in the Board on the subject, he returned the money to the donors.

" This was right and highly proper. It is just what ought to be done by all friends of the Slave. What! are we to be told by the Society that their field is the world—and then the Society make a bargain with the robbers of God's poor, stipulating that a part of the field shall be left unoccupied? Shall those whose legitimate business it is to supply the famishing with the bread of life, strike hand with cupidity and robbery, and make a bargain that certain millions shall starve and perish? Let those who have any bowels of compassion think of these things, and say whether they will ratify the foul bargain."—*Vermont Telegraph.*

HONOUR TO MR STEVENSON, THE AMERICAN MINISTER!

LETTER FROM JOSEPH STURGE, TO THE MEMBERS OF THE BRITISH ASSO-CIATION FOR THE ADVANCEMENT OF SCIENCE.

(*From the* BRITISH EMANCIPATOR.)

I OBSERVE in the Report of the proceedings at a dinner of the members of your body, on the 29th ult., at the Town-hall, in this place, where the Marquis of Northampton presided, Andrew Stevenson, the American minister, was treated with distinguished honour, and that in addressing the company he said :—

" America and England were bound together by strong and glorious ties—they were allied in blood, religion, habits, and associations—they worshipped the same God, and in the same manner."

While according, on this occasion, to the American minister that attention to which you might deem his position entitled him, you might be little disposed to criticise too closely the equivocal congratulations conveyed in this sentence, or to remember that there were "habits and associations" in Slave-dealing America, which it would be the deepest insult to insinuate applied to yourselves—I mean the American Slave Trade and Slavery, with which Andrew Stevenson is alike politically and personally identified.*

We may indeed lament, if the Atlantic should cease to sever us from the "habits" of iniquity and the degrading "associations" which this system involves. It would be an outrage to the feelings of Englishmen to suppose, that any ties could make them one with a community whose moral sense is so utterly extinguished as to insert advertisements similar to the following, in their public newspapers:—

"Twenty dollars reward.—Ran away, a negro man, named Harrison. It is supposed that he will make for South Carolina in *pursuit* of HIS WIFE, in possession of Captain D. Bird.

"CORNELIUS BEAZLY."

(From the *Florida Watchman*, Tallahasse, May 12, 1839. Motto,— "Principle and the People.")

"100 dollars is subscribed and will be punctually paid by the citizens of Onslow, to any person who may safely confine in any jail in this State, a certain negro man, named Alfred. The same reward will be paid, if satisfactory evidence is given of his having been KILLED; he has one or more scars caused by his having been shot.

"THE CITIZENS OF ONSLOW."

"Ran away, my negro man, named Richard. A reward of twenty-five dollars will be paid for his apprehension, DEAD or ALIVE. Satisfactory proof will only be required of his being KILLED. He has with him, in all probability, his wife Eliza, who ran away from Colonel Thompson, now a resident of Alabama, about the time he commenced his journey to that State.

"DURANT H. RHODES."

(From the *Wilmington (N. C.) Advertiser*, June 1, 1838. Motto,—"Be just and fear not.")

The only charge against these Negroes is endeavouring to obtain that liberty which they have never forfeited, and to which they have as much right as the American minister himself.

I rejoice in believing that the "mighty power of steam walking over the waters," making "neighbours of people who had never seen each other

---

* On the 1st of August last year, at a meeting to commemorate the Abolition of British Colonial Slavery, held in the same Town-hall, Daniel O'Connell said:—"It is asserted that their very ambassador is a Slave-breeder—one of those beings who rear and breed up Slaves for the purpose of traffic. Is it possible that America would send a man who traffics in blood, and who, if he do, would be a disgrace to human nature." This has not been denied by the American minister, and a letter from the Secretary of the American Anti-Slavery Society, dated from New York the 22d of November, 1838, states:—"The conduct of Mr Stevenson, of whom it is undeniable Mr O'Connell spoke only the truth, has been a standing subject of debate, even in the Slave States, and in the course of the discussion it cannot fail to have been seen by some, how intolerable is an institution which, though honourable at home, disgraces all connected with it abroad."

before," so justly the theme of Andrew Stevenson's praise, and the result of that skill and science it is the laudable object of your association to promote, will bear across the Atlantic such correct information of the horrors of the prison-house, that the actors in these scenes ere long will be regarded in the same light as the public robber or the midnight assassin. There is, however, a noble and rapidly increasing number in America who claim our aid, our sympathy, and prayers, associated in upwards of sixteen hundred societies, making strenuous efforts for the liberation of more than two millions five hundred thousand of their countrymen, found by the Slave-owner

> " Guilty of a skin
> Not coloured like his own ; and having power
> To enforce the wrong, for such a worthy cause
> Dooms and devotes him as a lawful prey.
> Chains him, and tasks him, and exacts his sweat
> With stripes, that mercy, with a bleeding heart,
> Weeps, when she sees inflicted on a beast."

We have happily lived to see the destruction of this accursed system in the British dominions, and every man of humanity would wish to lend all the legitimate aid in his power to those who are struggling for the same great object in other parts of the world. Are we not bound by this consideration to show all who are implicated in it, whatever station they may fill—that the only condition upon which they can share our hospitality, and receive from us the right hand of fellowship, is to let the " oppressed go free ? "

I am, very respectfully,

JOSEPH STURGE.

BIRMINGHAM, 9th month, 7th, 1839.

FORMATION OF ANTI-SLAVERY SOCIETIES

IN JAMAICA.

No. III.

No sooner had the Negroes tasted the sweets of Freedom, than they set about measures for extending the benefit to others. In Jamaica, a number of Societies have been formed, for promoting, in conjunction with the " British and Foreign Anti-Slavery Society" in London, the Abolition of Slavery *throughout the World*. The first of these—that at Falmouth— has already subscribed and remitted One Hundred Pounds to this country, for the furtherance of the general object; and on the 1st of August last, the Society celebrated their first Anniversary. At the same date, other Societies of a similar description were instituted. At Kingston, the Mayor presided; and respecting the Meeting, the amiable and Christian-minded Captain Stuart, says:—" It was a well attended, a very animated, and a very cordial meeting. All seemed fervently to sympathize in abol-ishing Slavery and the Slave Trade throughout the world. The spirit evinced exceeded the best expectations of the most thorough friends of Freedom, and of the best informed in the island. I think there is reason to hope that it will be an efficient Auxiliary. Two gentlemen, long not on speaking terms, shook hands heartily at the end of yesterday's meeting, and all this without the least compromise of principle. Indeed, I never heard Slavery more emphatically characterized as it is in other nations now, and was until recently here, than on that occasion; its guilt and horror were vividly depicted. These Auxiliaries, I trust, will spread throughout the island; and will, I am persuaded, powerfully exert a heal-ing and purifying influence *here*, besides bearing importantly upon the question all over the world."

At the formation of the St. Catherine's Branch Anti-Slavery Society, the Chair was occupied by Captain Stuart; and the following are the Patron and Office-Bearers :—*Patron*,—SIR LIONEL SMITH, BART. *President*,—THE HON. THOMAS JAMES BERNARD. *Vice-Presidents*,— THE HON. ALEXANDER BRAVO, WALTER GEORGE STEWART, WILLIAM THOMAS MARCH, and CHARLES HENRY DARLING, ESQS. *Secretary*,— LARCHIN LYNCH, ESQ. *Treasurer*,—THE REV. J. M. PHILLIPO, Bap-tist Missionary.

Extract of a letter from the Rev. John Clark, Baptist Missionary, dated Brown's Town, August 27th, 1839:—

" On the 1st of August, we formed the Brown's Town Auxiliary to the British and Foreign Anti-Slavery Society. The meeting was a spirited one ; Mr Simmons, the Wesleyan Minister, spoke eloquently on the subject. Mr Wheeler, of the Bible Society, gave an interesting address, and some of our *emancipated friends*, with much propriety of expression and ardent feeling, pressed upon their brethren and sisters the importance of their uniting with their good friends in England in attempting to bring about the Abolition of Slavery and the Slave Trade. The meeting was adjourned until September, when we hope to have Capt. Stuart and other friends with us, and to make a collection for the Anti-Slavery Society."

Of the formation of the St. Jago de-la-Vega Branch of the British and Foreign Anti-Slavery Society, the able Editor of the Jamaica *Colonial Reformer*, Dr. A. L. Palmer, (lately Editor of the *British Emancipator,*) thus writes:—

" The chapel was more crowded on this occasion than we ever recollect to have seen it. There could not have been fewer than fifteen hundred persons present: an assembly so varied was certainly never before within its walls ; all classes of society existing in this town and neighbourhood; all colours, all ages, all religious persuasions, and both sexes, were seen enthusiastically vieing with each other who should be foremost in the glorious career of humanity, justice, and brotherly love. We were particularly pleased at seeing many of the most respectable managers of properties in the parish rendering their aid in the great cause, not only by their presence and by their voices, but most liberally from their purses also! Who, then, shall say that there is no hope for Jamaica? It was one of the most heart-cheering and gratifying scenes we ever witnessed. We find ourselves, however, quite unable to give an adequate description of the animated proceedings—of the enthusiasm, unanimity, and good-will displayed by all parties at the meeting."

That lion-hearted defender of the coloured man, the Rev. William Knibb, amidst all the annoyances and persecution of the foes of Liberty, continues undauntedly to plead for the rights of the deeply harassed, though legally enfranchised Negroes. The following speech will be perused with the liveliest interest by every friend to the cause of Universal Freedom:—

SPEECH OF THE REV. WILLIAM KNIBB,

At the First Anniversary of the Falmouth Anti-Slavery Society,

August 1st, 1839.

" The Rev. W. Knibb rose to move the fifth Resolution, and said:—Mr Chairman and my Christian friends, there are very few ministers who can preach without a text, and I am glad you have given me one. I did not make this Resolution, but I am glad it has been made, and before I proceed to speak about it, I shall read it. It is as follows:—' That this meeting repels with indignation the false and atrocious accusations made, during the first year of freedom, against the labouring population by the slave tyrants of Jamaica, and dares the enemies of the Negro race to substantiate even one of those foul slanders which they are continually heaping upon it.'—Now, Mr Chairman, I am prepared to support this Resolution, and I do dare our enemies to substantiate any one of the numerous charges they have made. The fact is this, we have arrived at the time when the state of society is such that we must combine energy of character with calmness of manner. An opinion prevails that I am a violent man, and that I take hold of every straw that floats upon the stream of time to keep alive agitation. The truth is, I have come to the conclusion, after fifteen years' calm reflection, that Slavery is entirely destructive of every social tie. It is destructive to the temporal—it is destructive of the spiritual—and it is destructive of the intellectual state of man. It is from

a firm conviction of this nature that I have done whatever I have done for
you. It is not for me now to speak of the private virtues and the public
acts of those benevolent individuals who have laboured, and have laboured
successfully, to obtain you your freedom; but this I will say, I have done
all that lay in my power to secure you that freedom which I hope you
will have energy enough to keep. (Yes, yes.) I dare say some burlesque
will be made at our having a black man in the chair to-day, on account of
his want of education, though he can both read and write; but the charge
of ignorance among the emancipated peasantry comes with a bad grace
from those who were the *causers* of that great ignorance, and whose forefathers, a few centuries ago, were equally unlettered. And I can also tell
you, there was a time when many of the clergymen of the Established
Religion could not read their A, B, C; that this was the case in England,
aye, and in happy Scotland too, and that this state of ignorance was that
of the most prominent of the clergy. But it is not education alone (though
none can prize it more than I do,) that qualifies a man to fill the chair at a
public meeting like this. If education does not do more for the black
man than it has done for the white men of this country—at least, for four
out of every five white men in the country, it would prove a curse rather
than a blessing. The same God that made the white, made the black
man. (Hear, hear.) The same blood that runs in the white man's veins,
flows in yours. (Hear, hear.) It is not the complexion of the skin, but the
complexion of character, that makes the great difference between one man
and another. (Cheers.) But to the Resolution—one charge brought against
you is this. Your enemies say the Baptists won't work. (It's false.) If
the Baptists never work, who helps to make all the sugar that is made?
(The Baptists.) Who helps to make all the rum? (The Baptists.) Yet
the Baptists never work. ('Tis a lie.) If the Baptists never work, I
should like to know where you got those fine bonnets and coats from, so
many of which I see here. Did you steal them? (No, no, no.) Did
you buy them? (Yes.) And pay for them? (Yes.) And with your
own money, (Yes,) which you worked for? (Yes.) But Mr Dyer says
you don't work. Mr Dyer says you won't work. (He is a liar.) Well,
I don't understand how you manage to get on so well, unless you worked,
and worked hard too for it. Indeed, I will defy the world to produce a
more respectably dressed peasantry than fill this chapel at this moment,
and out of the good staunch Anti-Slavery men and women within these
walls, I fearlessly assert, that there is not one who either stole the clothing
he wears, or who has not paid, by his own industry, the merchant of whom
he purchased it.

"But who is this modern Solon, who is for ever traducing the honest and
industrious labourer? What are the qualifications he possesses, who, in
this town, sends out his weekly bulletin of the state of public morals?—
The immaculate William Dyer!!! On his noble structure nature has
exhausted her energies, while his mind, fraught with every lofty sentiment,
has ever disdained the least semblance of falsehood or detraction. Whether
we view his private character, or his public acts, we are lost in admiration.
Purity sits enthroned upon his majestic brow, and vice recedes as she witnesses his magnanimous career. Talk not to me of Demosthenes, speak
not of the noble-minded Milton—let all the mighty spirits of by-gone days
retire! Where worth is respected, where manly courage is revered, there
let William Dyer's name be as a talisman to whom youth shall look with
respect, and age itself revere. (Roars of laughter.) Who dares even
whisper that such a person could err, that malice could rankle in his breast!
What! Mr Dyer says that which is not true? Impossible! Mr Dyer

never told a falsehood. And yet Mr Dyer said that Richard Williams, who committed the robbery at Sievwright's, was a Baptist. ('Tis false.) Mr Dyer said I would even receive stolen money. (He lies.) But Mr Dyer says so in his paper, and his is really a choice paper; the articles in his paper are as refreshing to me as so many mouthfuls of ice cream. (Laughter.) I have one of his papers here now, and I'll tell you what he published only yesterday.—Here it is—pray listen to it.—' *Knibb, formerly a baker in Devizes, and Oughton, a decayed upholsterer, appeared to be the leading men of this mischievous sect, and now keep their carriages and live in great splendour in Jamaica. Upon two occasions Knibb brought* 10,000 *men into a small town, to the great alarm of the inhabitants, without the Governor interfering or checking his audacity.'* Now, to think of printing this in the very town where every one knows it is false! It is such an act of folly and absurdity that I wonder any paper in England would insert it. Yet, Mr Dyer is a good man—an honourable man—a truth-telling man—a respectable man—and let him gainsay it who dare.

"Another question I shall refer to, is this. Your enemies say you won't pay rent for your houses; but let us see what is the rent they wish to charge. Why, they charge the husband, the wife, and every one of the children in a family, rent for a miserable hut and patch of land. I should be happy if you could enter into arrangements at once to pay a fair rent for your houses and grounds; but I should say, if you pay the rent they wish to charge you would be great fools. If the attorneys will come forward in a spirit of fairness, I will recommend you to pay rent at once. But if John Jackson, and Mary Jackson, and Wilberforce Jackson, and Buxton Jackson, and Sir Lionel Smith Jackson, and all the rest of the little Jacksons, are each to be charged rent for a house and an acre of land, they would be great fools indeed to pay it. (Cheers.) I say, let the Planters know you are freemen, and that you wish to be treated as freemen. (Yes.) Tell them you must be treated as every other freeman is. (Yes.) I should say, you ought not to engage to rent your houses for a short time; but quarterly or yearly. You may pay the rental weekly, or monthly, or quarterly, for short accounts are best, but you must not suffer yourselves to be taken in by any arrangements which you do not fully understand: ask advice, and I am sure you will get it. If the Planters acted properly I am sure there would be no necessity for me to say one word to you about it; the fact is, they do not wish to act properly. There are some honourable men, I know, among them, who will act fairly; but it is my firm conviction that there are attorneys in Jamaica, who would bring you back again to Slavery if they could. (Yes, yes.) And are we always to be persecuted thus, and are we never to speak? They say every thing they like against us, and are we never to stand on our own defence? The senior Magistrate of this parish went last week to the commanding officer at the garrison, and insulted the whole population, by asking him to prepare the troops to turn out against us, *for there was to be a rebellion.* (Oh! oh!) And are we never to be allowed to speak? And if I don't stand up to defend you, who in Falmouth will do it for you? (None!) Well then, since we have no protection to expect from them, we must combine our energies, constitutionally to protect ourselves. (Cheers.) There are infamous laws existing in the Island, which we must try to get abolished. One of them was alluded to in the House of Commons not long ago, by the Secretary for the Colonies. It is to this effect:—' All rogues, vagabonds, or other idle persons found wandering from place to place, or otherwise disorderly, may be apprehended by the constable, and taken before a Magistrate, who is empowered to order him or her to be whipped on the naked back, not exceeding thirty-nine lashes.' (Hear, hear.) Another clause makes it lawful to send any coloured person who comes within the description of the Act to the parish work-house, to be set to work any time not exceeding six months; but all white persons committed shall be fed, lodged, and worked, separate and apart from the free Negroes, Mulattoes, and Slaves. Suppose a person like one whom I could name, who is so well known for the tender mercies he possesses, were to see my deacon, Mr Brown, or his wife, upon his property, some day just after he had had his dinner, and should order his constable to take hold of them as idle vagabonds, and lay them down, and give them each thirty-nine lashes, would that be right? (No.) Is that the way freemen are to be treated. (No, no.) Ought such a law as that to exist? (No, no, no.) No, my friends, it ought not; and I will never rest till it is repealed. You will bear in mind that this statute makes it lawful to send any coloured person, who comes within this description of the Act, to the work-house, to be set to work for any time, not exceeding six months;—but all white persons committed for the same offences are to be fed, lodged, and worked, separate and apart from the free Negroes, Mulattoes, and Slaves. This law, my friends, makes the distinction of complexion the rule for the measure of punishment. The white man, or the white female, who is taken up as a vagrant, is to be fed, lodged, and accommodated, with comparative comfort; but the black man, or the black female, is to be subjected to the withering influence of cruelty, and to all the agonies that may be inflicted by the accursed cart-whip. (Oh! oh! Hear, hear.) But this law was never made for freemen; it was made for the Slave. Send it to Cuba;—send it to America, or anywhere else you please, but it won't do for Jamaica! If it is good for the black man, it is good for the white man. My opinion is, that every law that makes any reference to colour at all, ought instantly to be repealed. But if they are so fond of it, let the white man be tried by it. Let one of them try it, and let one of my drivers lay it on; and then let him say whether it is fair, and just, and proper. (Laughter.) But the law says, it is the black man and the Mulatto who is to be so treated—is that justice? (No, no.) Yes, it is Jamaica justice. (Hear, hear.)

" They will perhaps ask: how does it happen that these laws are not enforced? I will tell you, it is not from any leniency on their parts, but from the prudence and foresight of our esteemed Governor, Sir Lionel Smith. I have it from good authority, that Sir Lionel Smith said he would dismiss the first magistrate that made use of this terrible engine to oppress the people. The fact is, there is no chance of our obtaining justice in Jamaica. In the case of myself, my church, and Mr Dyer, the Attorney-General told the Jury I had no wish to punish Mr Dyer, nor any other individual, by legal penalties. I only wished to vindicate myself and my church from the foul and atrocious assertion made against us by Mr Dyer, the organ of the Planters. But there was no justice to be obtained: what confidence, then, can we have in prejudiced, political, perjured Juries? (Hear, hear.) Now, our confidence is at home. In England we have powerful influence, if not here: I have sent the Report of the trial of Mr Dyer home, to vindicate my character, and the character of my people, and to prove to the British public that there is no justice in Jamaica for any man that hates Slavery.

" Your enemies say there is no sugar made this year: then I should like to know what were those ships loaded with that sailed out of the harbour during the last two months? (' Sweet sand, sweet sand,' accompanied by roars of laughter.) *I am informed that there will not be a sufficient number of ships to carry home the sugar that has been cultivated; if so, what* becomes of all their loud complaints? The Planters raised a terrible hue and cry about the estates being all turned into ruinate. I should like to know how it is there are no estates to sell? (Laughter.) I want to buy a fine estate, do you know any ruined estates for sale? (Cheers, and cries of ' No, no.') Well, then, let them say on. I defy them all to substan. tiate one single charge which they have made against the Baptists. I tell them fearlessly that there is not a more peaceful, clean, orderly, and indus. trious people on the earth : and I challenge them to prove the contrary. It is not in this Chapel alone I would face them. Let them have a public meeting at the Court-House, and let them have their say, and let me have mine ; and I'll pledge myself to prove every assertion I have made, and I defy the whole of the calumniators of the Baptist Church to prove a single charge they have made against us. O, that they would come forward in their proper persons, and not under the assumed garb of ' Spectators' and ' Natives,' and I know not what! (Laughter.) Never was there a single soul of them who came forward to contradict our statements, but one who suddenly jumped into the matter, and as quickly jumped out again. (Im- mense laughter at this allusion to Mr Jump.) They perhaps think them- selves so important, and ourselves so unworthy of notice, that they will not stoop to answer us ; then, upon their principles, I should like to know why they do take so much notice of us? (Hear.) There is not a paper in the island but what teems with my name. (Hear.) If you look over any of them you find a few thousand Knibbs, (A laugh,) and you will find that Knibb is dubbed a Pope, a Mahomet, an Agitator, a Dan O'Connell, and I know not what. (Immense cheering.) If we are so insignificant, why do they then notice us? Why do they not let us alone? I'll tell you what it is. They know that we have power. They know that we have influence here and power at home. I am not afraid to tell them all my mind. They shall not taunt me and say, that I said in England what I dared not to say here. I met the advocates of Slavery in England. I met and faced their great champion, Mr Peter Borthwick ; and now I am here, and am not afraid to say here what I said in England. Where are my enemies? Let me see them—let them come forward. Why don't they do this? (Because they are afraid.) One thing that you will have to think of is this, that you provide yourselves with medicines and obtain proper medical advice, and from gentlemen of proper character. I hope the members of my church will choose men of moral character to visit their families ; there are such men to be found, whom I hope they will always prefer. I do not choose for you—choose for yourselves. There is thrown around this soul of mine such a love of liberty, that were I to have my will I would have every one free ; and my most fervent wish is, that wherever the sun shines every one should be emancipated, and made as free as I am. I cannot conclude without congratulating this meeting on this first Anniversary of their freedom. I wish you joy, and I hail you happy in the enjoyment of this great blessing. When I reflect upon the circumstance, that 300,000 human beings have been set free in this island, and not one has ever raised his hand to strike a white man, I can- not but rejoice that the moral influence of religion has been so manifest. Do not, my dear friends, ever allow yourselves to be betrayed into any acts of violence. Continue to act consistently and honestly, according to the word of God. If you want advice under any circumstances, ask it, and depend upon it you will get it. Under the present circumstances in which you are placed by the laws to which I have alluded, you may depend upon it that the lion of Great Britain has only to lay his paw upon these iniqui- tous laws, and they shall be annihilated at once. All that we want is equal justice; the same justice for the black that there is for the white man; that a man is not to be punished because he is black. I here pledge myself that I will not rest till you are placed upon the same footing as I am. I will not be satisfied till your wives are placed upon the same footing as my wife. (Cheers.) If I were a black man, I should not be ashamed of the colour of my skin. (Hear him.) There is no disgrace in being black. (No, no.) I did not make myself white. God made me as I am, and he made you as you are. (Yes.) There are some persons, I am told, who have been what is termed white-washed: that is, they paid a sum of money to the House of Assembly, and were christened white, but the colour would not stand, and they soon turned yellow again. (Great laughter.) Well, then, my friends, I again hail you free, and I wish you joy on this Anniversary of your freedom. I do rejoice that you have not only borne calumny and reproach, with a Christian spirit, but that you have learnt to forgive your enemies.—Now, then, three cheers for the Queen."

Three cheers being given with all the ardour of their hearts, the Rev. Gentleman sat down amid the loudest acclamations of the people.

NOTE.—The following is from the *Colonial Gazette*, of Aug. 28th, 1839, published in London, a Journal devoted exclusively to the interests of the Colonies, and may therefore be deemed pretty good authority on the subject quoted. Under the head "Colonial Markets," it is said—"The Stock is now approximating that of last year at this period, and there seems to be little doubt but that at the end of the year *there will be more West India Sugar in the warehouses than for many years past;* arising from the great decrease in the consumption of the article, occasioned chiefly by high prices which have been supported under the impression that there would be a very material decrease in the production of Sugar in the West Indies this year. Of Mauritius, the stock is very large, and greatly exceeds that of last year."

The *North British Advertiser*, of Nov. 30th, says, "The Gazette average price (of Sugar) is now 38s. 6d. In 1838, it was 31s. 3½d.; and in 1837, 41s. 11d.—The Stock of British Plantation Sugar is now 39,198 hhds. and tierces, which is 2,294 more than last year at the same period."

So much for the Negroes not working! The falling off in crops !! and the *ruinous effects* of Emancipation !!! so assiduously propagated and promulgated by the Plantocracy—while, as regards the *price* of Sugar, it appears it is *not so high* as in 1837, the last year of the glorious Apprenticeship, or British Enacted Imperial Slavery.

Surely these statements, independent of any other, are an effectual contradiction to Colonial falsehoods.

ABORIGINES PROTECTION SOCIETY.

No. IV.

ON Tuesday evening, the 15th October, 1839, a public meeting was held in the Rev. Dr. Wardlaw's Chapel, chiefly for the purpose of hearing an Address from Sir Culling Eardley Smith, Bart., on the Objects of the Aborigines Protection Society; but likewise for addressing Memorials to Government relative to the Negroes captured in the Amistad, and praying that the Independence of Texas should not be recognised.

On the motion of the Rev. Greville Ewing, W. P. Paton, Esq., was called to the Chair. In opening the business,

The CHAIRMAN thanked the Meeting for the honour they had done him in calling upon him to preside on the present occasion. It always gave him great pleasure to meet with the inhabitants of Glasgow on a subject so interesting as the Emancipation of the Negro race. He had, however, no expectation of such an honour as that now conferred upon him, and was therefore unprepared with any address. He might state that the Glasgow Emancipation Society had taken the opportunity of a visit made to this quarter by Sir C. E. Smith to request him to address them on the objects of the Aborigines Protection Society. About twelve months ago, the inhabitants of this city were addressed on the same subject by Mr Montgomery Martin and Mr George Thompson, and it was then resolved by the Emancipation Society to co-operate with the Aborigines Society, and to give it all the aid in their power. Since that period, however, it has been but little that the Committee could do for the support of that institution, owing chiefly to the Glasgow Society being in debt to a large amount, arising from the struggle they were called upon to maintain against the Negro Apprenticeship system in our colonies. (Cheers.) The Committee, however, had no doubt that they would be supported by the approbation of the people of Glasgow, and trusted that it would be in their power to render more efficient assistance to the Society in London. (Cheers.) In addition to the Hon. Baronet, they would that night have the pleasure of hearing a gentleman from Canada (Dr. Rolph,) who took a deep interest in their proceedings at Glasgow. (Cheers.)

Sir C. E. SMITH then addressed the meeting. He expressed the great pleasure he felt in being called upon to address so respectable a meeting, on so interesting a subject as the Aborigines Society. He wished, however, that the gentlemen who had taken the management of the meeting had not, in so prominent a manner, announced that he was to deliver " an address," for the expression seemed to imply that he was better prepared with details than he really was. He had not had the opportunity that Mr George Thompson had of making himself acquainted with the whole of the details, and was therefore not so well prepared to address them as the announcement which had been made might lead the meeting to suppose.

The Aborigines Society was one in which he took a deep interest, and whose meetings he had occasionally attended; and when it was known to that Society that he was proceeding to Scotland, a wish was expressed that he should put himself in communication with the local committees, a request which he complied with most willingly, and was therefore ready to lay before them such facts as were in his possession, connected with the objects of the Society. (Loud cheering.) It might be necessary for him to state that the general object of the Aborigines Society was the protection of the aboriginal inhabitants not only of our own colonies, but, so far as their influence could be brought to bear, of the original inhabitants of other colonies also. (Cheers.) If he were to use another word in place of the aborigines, he would say the "unprotected," for their society was intended to protect those who had no means of protecting themselves. (Cheers.) And if any subdivisions of that great class, a class which always had, and ever would command the sympathies of the British public—if any subdivision of that class were put out of the sphere of their operations, it was not because they did not feel an interest in these classes, but because they had already recognised protectors of their own. For instance, when Mr George Thompson was advocating the cause of the Aborigines Society throughout the country, he found, and others also found, that, not only from the number of the persons affected, but from the greatness of the interests affected, and the way those interests came home to the bosoms of the inhabitants of this country, that the Aborigines of India involved a subject so large that it prevented him from sufficiently alluding to the other classes included in the objects of this Society; and the result of that circumstance had been, that, so great was the interest felt in reference to British India, that a separate Society was formed with regard to India alone. (Hear.) He was far from regretting this circumstance—indeed he rejoiced in it; and if, therefore, he did not allude at length to India that night, it was not because he did not feel a great interest in the affairs of India, but because the people of India had already protectors of their own. He thought they had a peculiar claim upon us, and that a strong case of cruelty could be made out against the Government in relation to India; and he regretted to see within these two days that the argument about the land-tax, and in behalf of the people of India, had been met by portions of the press, designed liberal, with the statement that the original tenure of Land in all countries was, that it was the property of the Government, and that the Government considered it a fund from which all the necessities of the State should be drawn. He was sorry to see a statement like that put forth, and the tenure of property in Europe contrasted with the tenure of property as it existed in India, as if they were very different things. (Hear.) There was another class who, in the strict understanding of the term, might be included under the name of Aborigines—he alluded to the Negro inhabitants of the West Indies; but their interests had too long had a claim on the sympathies of the British people—they had too long found unyielding and ardent defenders in the people of Glasgow, and the circumstances of that class were too well known to the inhabitants of this city to render it necessary for him to dwell on the subject. (Hear, hear, hear.) But, as he said of India, so he said of the emancipated Negroes—it was not because they were not included in his subject—it was not because he had not a deep interest in their welfare—it was not because, that from Slaves they had become apprentices, and from apprentices freemen—it was not because of their transition from one name to another, that, therefore, this class should cease to command their sympathies, or to require their assistance to the uttermost. No. When the defenders of that class found, that though no longer Slaves, they were yet harassed by every description of litigation—though no longer oppressed in the name of Slavery, yet were oppressed by every means in the power of their former taskmasters—having their wages violently depressed, deprived of their provision grounds, and difficulties of every kind thrown in the way of their emigration from one island to another—obstacles thrown in the way of the administration of justice—the exertions of Parliament, for the improvement of the people, thwarted by those who, though they had ceased to be the enemies, had not ceased to be the oppressors of the Negroes—when the defenders of the Negro found this, they could not cease to take a deep interest in his protection. They would perhaps now ask him, who were those whom the Society undertook to protect? He would say, in general terms, that the classes they sought to protect were those in every locality where civilized came into contact with uncivilized people. (Loud cheering.) If they had not history to tell them of the danger to which these classes were exposed, they might, with great saftey, draw *a priori* an argument, as to the usage they would receive, from what they knew of human nature. The Hon. Baronet then went on to show more fully that, on the principles of human nature, the uncivilized portion of mankind might be expected to be exposed to oppression; and this was fully borne out by the facts of history. After a reference to the atrocities committed by Europeans in South America, he said he might direct them to the colonies now peopled by the recently emancipated Negroes, and remind them, that that race had succeeded another race, of whom not a single individual now remained—that, in short, not one of the original race in the West Indies now existed on the soil. Again, he might refer to Newfoundland, where, literally, within the last six years, the last aboriginal inhabitant was shot by a colonist, so that not one of the original inhabitants of Newfoundland was now to be found. He stated these facts with a view to show that the inference they might deduce from their knowledge of human nature was completely borne out by the facts of history. (Hear, hear.) But perhaps he would be asked if there were no facts more recent than these—"these statements are no doubt of deep interest—you allude to topics heart-rending in their character, but the races of which you speak are exterminated, the circumstances have ceased to exist, and have now no particular interest:"—But, unfortunately, history not only recorded the extermination of tribes, but the intelligence received from month to month, and from year to year, distinctly showed that human nature was the same still, and that where public opinion and the influence of righteous laws were not brought to bear, uncivilized tribes were subjected to the same oppressions, and the same foul influences which they had read were inflicted in the worst times of Spanish and Portuguese oppression. (Cheers.) If it should be said, that the tone of society in the world was now so much improved that it would be only reasonable to expect that similar atrocities as before would not now be perpetrated, he had simply to ask, if the South Sea Islands had found that the boasted character of modern European nations had preserved them from acts of oppression, the contemplation of which made the blood run cold. He would quote the authority of Mr Williams to show that not only before that excellent missionary went to the South Sea, but since, acts of the kind he had referred to had often been committed in these islands. A European vessel touches at one of the South Sea Islands, and lands some of the crew for the purpose of barter. Perhaps the very thing they import, the intoxicating liquors they bring with them, become the cause of a quarrel, and the origin of all the evils that follow. In a state of intoxication a dispute arises—blood flows, and the remainder of the crew returns to their ship. What would be the conduct of a really civilized Captain in such circumstances? To detect the criminal, whether among his own men or among the natives, and see that justice is done; but instead of this, in nine cases out of ten, the ship sails round the island, perhaps a distance of 20 miles, finds a lot of harmless individuals collected on its shores, and the crew of the ship fires upon these, and kills a number of them. (Hear.) Another ship visits the island; and the natives, less irrationally than might be supposed, connect this ship with the last, take the initiative in the quarrel, and attack the ship; feelings of irritation thus begun, are kept up, and often end with the extermination of large tribes of the inhabitants. He was not there to defend savages, because they took vessels and committed acts of outrage upon the crews; but he must observe, that if the civilized would only act as Christian and civilized men ought to do, the evil would, in a great measure, be averted: and it was to cases of that sort that the Aborigines Society desired to bring the influence of local colonial governments to bear, as well as the moral influence of all who were likely to be concerned for the perpetration of such atrocities. (Cheers.) But it might be said that he only spoke of the South Sea Islands, over which our Government had no colonial control; he would, therefore, come nearer home, and refer them to Van Diemen's Land, where, within the last 20 years, there were four distinct aboriginal tribes of inhabitants. Within that period more than one half of these inhabitants had been exterminated by European violence, a small remnant of them only remained, and these few had been removed by an excellent and philanthropic individual to a place of refuge in Bass's Straits. Even within the last three or four years— nay, within the last 12 months—similar atrocities had been committed in the populous colony of Eastern Australia. He now quoted the authority of a gentleman who had recently returned from Australia, he meant Dr. Lang, who stated that, in consequence of the Government of Australia having taken notice of attacks made by convicts and others on the natives, it was notorious that some of the leading colonists there had said that, if their servants were prohibited taking advantage of the inhabitants in the way they had previously done, they would do so by mixing poison with their bread. (Sensation.) This threat had been made within the last 12 months, and he stated it on the authority of Dr. Lang. He would not longer dwell upon these isolated cases, but direct them to two or three points in which the Society had been specially interested within the last few weeks, and therefore he requested them to follow him to the colony of the Cape. He should also have directed them to Canada, were it not that another gentleman would afterwards speak with more knowledge on that subject, so interesting to the inhabitants of Glasgow. He (Sir C. E. Smith) would likewise refer to a subject that could not fail to interest the inhabitants of this city: and in which he believed the views of many right-minded philanthropists in London entirely coincided with the views entertained in Glasgow—he alluded to New Zealand. He was happy to know that the colony about to be carried to that country would be conducted on principles not only conducive to the welfare and safety of those who go there, but also for the protection of the natives. (Cheers.) Perhaps he might be addressing some who were not acquainted with the circumstances of the Cape colony, and for their information he would allude to matters which might perhaps be familiarly known to others. The Cape was originally a Dutch settlement, though it had now become the property of the English, and had a mixed population, partly of Dutch, British, and other nations— besides uncivilized tribes with whom they were brought into contact. Of the capacities of these tribes, under right training and civilizing influences, he had had ample proof from conversation with missionaries from that country. Within the last few months he had seen Mr Moffat, a mission. ary, who had returned from the country, and who assured him that, among the young men connected with his Christian society, there were persons with abilities and talents calculated to make them shine in any civilized society, and every inquiry that could be made into the character of the natives of South Africa, much as their appearance might lead superficial observers to think otherwise, proved that they were capable of doing what any other class of men could perform—as much so as were the inhabitants of the West Indies, whose capabilities had been so satisfactorily proved. (Cheers.) For many years, the Dutch farmers, or boors, at the Cape Town settlement, had been discontented with the English Government. He was not going to call up old sores, or to inquire whether these discon. tents were justifiable or unjustifiable, but so it was, they were much dissatis. fied with the Government; and with one thing, he grieved to say, they were especially dissatisfied—the emancipation of the Slaves—though for these Slaves the most ample compensation had been made. One circumstance conspiring with another (observed the Hon. Baronet) had induced large bodies of men to go from the colony and commit acts of outrage and riot on the native tribes; and not only had they committed these acts of aggres- sion upon the natives, but they had carried off a large number of Slaves, for whose emancipation they had received an ample recompense from the British public. A flagrant case of this kind had occurred within the last three months, a report of which was given to the Aborigines Society by a gentleman, whose name was familiar to all, and one who was revered and respected wherever known, he meant Sir John Herschell. (Cheers.) It appeared that a body of these men, while proceeding to another part of the country, invaded the territory of a tribe, whose chief, being apprised of the emigration, had threatened that, if any body of men, from whatever quarter, should enter his territory, he would regard it as an act of hostility. A collision took place between the invaders and the subjects of this native chieftain, and the consequence was, that the tribe had been all but exter- minated. To show how completely the tribe had been ruined, an African mission established in that country had been obliged to quit, because the population had actually disappeared before their eyes. (Hear.) The emigrants passed through the country and occupied the country of Port Natan, the territory of another native Prince. He believed they would all be acquainted with the history of Capt. Gardiner, who took a large tract of land in the country from this chieftain, and who, it appeared, put up the land for sale at different prices, and made some conveyance of the land to these emigrants. However, these boors had taken possession of this country, and were perpetrating great acts of cruelty and outrage towards the natives. Now, the Aborigines Society felt that the English Govern- ment were bound to interfere in this case. Within our territory, the natives were exterminated, and if there was one thing more than an- other called for in international law, it was, that protection should be given in all cases where there was submission to British law. The Hon. Baronet next briefly adverted to Canada, and expressed his satis- faction that, according to the latest intelligence, the Colonial Govern- ment was now persevering in an improved course of policy towards the natives. The old practice of removing the natives whenever it suited Eu- ropean policy, was now altered, and measures were taken for the protection of the natives, and for promoting their civilization. This part of the sub- ject would, however, be much better laid before them by the gentleman who was that night to address them. Passing over Canada, then, and going to New Zealand, he must repeat that he rejoiced to find there was now a probability of that difficult problem being settled, how it was possible for emigration to be beneficial, combined with the due and proper protection of the natives. If he was addressing any who were likely, in a few days, to go to New Zealand, he might say that they were going to a colony to be conducted on a principle as sound as any in the British dominions. He trusted that, if the proposition were made to send a colony, in violation, or in defiance of natural rights, to New Zealand, there would not be held up a hand in its favour. But in New Zealand it was very different from this. We had no longer there, as it were, a sheet of white paper, on which any thing might be marked, but we had a place, where, like it as we might, European influence would be brought to bear. We had to deal with a colony where already a good many settlers were located: and here he would quote from the authority of Dr. Lang, who left Australia early this year, whose accounts come down as late as the month of February, and whose statements must therefore interest all who were anxious for the prosperity of the natives of the country. Dr. Lang states that among the settlers of New Zealand there are many persons of respectable character, but many also of the worst character, some of them run-away sailors and convicts from the penal settlements of Australia, runaway debtors, and mere adventurers known in the phraseology of the country by the name of land-sharks,—persons who endeavour to extort land at the cheapest rate from the natives, that they may sell it again at an extravagant profit. It was no longer possible to say that Europeans shall not settle there. The only question was, how shall you deal with a society where such injurious materials exist? Dr. Lang related many cases of cruelty, oppression, and contempt of law among the settlers. In these circumstances, and when it was considered that there was no strong government there, it was not matter of surprise that such excesses as had been stated should occur. He mentioned one instance of a French Captain of a vessel hiring some English sailors, with whose character he was not acquainted. These persons, it appeared, had incurred some heavy debts in a public-house of the lowest description; the owners of which seized the captain's whaling boat, and carried it away, and thus kept him from putting to sea. In these circumstances, the only means that could be resorted to in the absence of law was to proceed to the public-house, and threaten that, if the whaling boat was not given up, the house would be pulled into the sea. The means of gaining land in that colony was very commonly this :—A person arrives, perhaps from Sydney, with muskets, powder, &c., and with a small stock of articles of this sort, in a few years he becomes master of large tracts of country ; so that the natives are literally wheedled out of their land for the veriest trifles. And this kind of extortion is, unfortunately, not confined to those from whom such acts might have been expected, but is also practised by persons whose professed object is the improvement of the natives. Before mentioning who they were to whom he alluded, he must state that he had a sincere respect for, and attachment to, the Society which sent these individuals to that country, and he believed that such acts had been committed without the knowledge of those by whom they had been commissioned. He alluded to the missionaries of the Church Missionary Society ; and he must observe, that he could not have believed the statements given, had they not been stated on such high authority as he had referred to. These missionaries had, however, been to a great extent the cause of the evils existing in New Zealand. (Hear.) They had become possessed of considerable tracts of land; the case of Mr Sheppard was mentioned, who, for a small consideration, had become the possessor of an estate having four miles of frontage along one of the rivers of New Zealand; and another gentleman, named Fairbairn, a missionary, was in possession of an estate with 35 miles of frontage. (Hear.) He was astonished that missionaries should so far forget the true policy, and the proper course to be pursued by them under their circumstances, and proceed in a way so much calculated to throw obstacles in the way of their own usefulness. When they so far forget their duty as to appropriate large tracts of land in this way, it was not surprising that persons of inferior character looked upon it as a warrant for them to proceed in a similar manner. (Great cheering.) He knew that there were societies whose instructions to their missionaries prevented them taking part in these transactions. (Cheers.) When he mentioned that the Wesleyan Missionaries, whose usefulness had doubled, ay, trebled that of the other, because they abstained from such acts; and when he knew that societies acting upon this principle had been able to associate with them far more members than the Church Missionary Society, which was carried on at an expence of £15,000 a year, had been able to do, he could see that that society had not only been acting contrary to every principle of justice, but to the policy that ought to have regulated its missionaries. (Cheers.) After referring to the great fertility and capabilites of New Zealand, the Hon. Baronet said, he was glad to find that her Majesty's Government, concurring in the recommendation of Dr. Lang, had decided to pursue a course which, while it would protect honest settlers, would also protect the interests of the native inhabitants. (Cheers.) After stating the established maxim, that the discoverers of a country were, by the laws of nations, first entitled to settle there, and that they had the right of preemption in all such cases, the Hon. Baronet observed that, in reference to New Zealand, Government had the right to interfere and insist on this right; and he rejoiced that it was the intention to do so, not to the injury of the honest settlers, who would be provided with better titles, but in the case of those who had acquired land in a nefarious manner, by the sort of transaction he had described, and who would be compelled, if they retained the land, to pay a fair price for it. (Cheers.) He rejoiced to think that a colony was likely to proceed from Scotland. Under the circumstances he had just stated, such a colony would not only be beneficial to our own country, but would be conducive to the interests of the native inhabitants. (Cheers.) It would fail him to tell all that the Aborigines Society was interesting itself about; but there was one thing he could not omit. It had long been a principle making way in this country that persons who could not, in a court of justice, conscientiously take an oath, should be allowed to give evidence with an affirmation. Such had been the case with the Society of Friends, who were always found at their posts when the cause of philanthropy was concerned, and the same benefit had been extended to other religious professions in the country; but the same privilege had not been given to the native inhabitants of our colonies, who, from their want of knowledge of the Scriptures, were unable to take an oath in a court of justice. The inconvenience of this had been often felt, even by Europeans, where the protection of property was concerned; and he had heard of a case of murder where the criminal escaped because a native witness was unable to take an oath, though no doubt existed as to his guilt. He trusted, therefore, that a measure would be obtained to enable the natives of our colonies to give evidence by affirmation. (Cheers.) Perhaps it might be asked, in what way the Aborigines Society interfered with such cases of oppression as came before them. They had, he would answer, frequent occasion to memorialise the Government, and had interviews with the heads of departments in the Government on such questions as they took up, besides communicating with Members of Parliament, and inducing them to attend to the discussion of these matters in the House. They had also made use of the Press, and from time to time had promulgated special papers on particular subjects. The Hon. Baronet then pointed out the claims which the Aborigines Society had upon Scotland and the North of England, from the circumstance that considerable expenditure had been made in advocating the views of the Society over the country, while that very advocacy, as in the case of Mr Thompson, had been followed by the institution of British India Societies. He rejoiced that such societies had been formed, but still their very formation gave the Aborigines Society a claim upon their cordial support. In conclusion, he showed the propriety of such a society existing in London, and called upon the people of Glasgow to unite, with the same energy, in behalf of the Aborigines of our other Colonies, as they had exhibited in the case of the Negroes of the West Indies. The Hon. Baronet then sat down amid loud cheering.

Dr. ROLPH, from Canada, was then called upon to address the meeting. He spoke nearly as follows:—Having recently arrived in this country from Upper Canada, and having been intrusted with an important negociation with her Majesty's Government, on behalf of an interesting, improving, and valuable class of persons in that province—I mean its coloured population—I trust I shall stand excused for directing the attention of this meeting to some matters intimately connected with its philanthropic objects.— (Cheers.) They are, perhaps, the most interesting fragment of American people to be found on the Continent of America. It has been long my happiness to watch their progress, and observe that, when treated with humanity and justice—as fortunately they have been in that colony—they have proved a grateful, honest, industrious, temperate, independent, and loyal people. (Cheers.) It may be interesting to this audience to know that their number, in the province of Upper Canada, is not less than 10,000, and chiefly from the great prison-house of Southern bondage. Since the foul and atrocious usurpation of Texas, the most daring and abominable robbery ever perpetrated, they feel their situation in Upper Canada unsafe; they see that the same means have been put into operation in that province as was pursued in Texas, and with the view to produce the like results. Kidnapping has been resorted to—they have been claimed under forced construction of international law, and they feel convinced, as every one must who has resided on the American Continent, that the annexation of Texas to the Southern States is not only contemplated, but resolved on, with a view to the rigid and permanent ascendancy of the Slave States. A few years ago, a number of Americans emigrated to the Mexican territories, under the specious pretence of settling there—called themselves Texians—declared themselves an oppressed people—well knowing that " the sympathy" of the vast Republic would be enlisted in their favour. (Hear, hear.) Although every other people wondered where the oppression was, the Americans, with an eagle eye, perceived it, and sent hundreds and thousands of their people, in organised bodies, to rescue from such unheard of tyranny the poor inoffensive Texians of from eight years to two months' standing. Previous to wresting that province from the Mexican States, the Southern press, for some time prior to the outbreak in that province, declared, and it has ever since unblushingly declared, that but for the Anti-Slavery law of Mexico that country would furnish an excellent market for their surplus—that the breeding state of Virginia would become more valuable—and it held out constant inducements to the speculators in human flesh, the man-merchants of the South, to open a trade

M

direct from the African coast to Mexico. The great, the immediate cause of the chivalry of the South, was to make a slave-market of Texas. This object having been now partially obtained, they looked with abhorrence on the British possessions in Upper Canada, where the fugitive slave was kindly welcomed and safely guarded. For some years past, the wretched being whom the Christian master of the land of liberty

> " Finds guilty of a skin
> Not coloured like his own; and having power
> To enforce the wrong, for such a worthy cause
> Dooms and devotes him as his lawful prey:
> Chains him, and tasks him, and exacts his sweat
> With stripes, that Mercy, with a bleeding heart,
> Weeps, when she sees inflicted on a beast,"

has found a city of refuge in Canada, under the banner of Britain. Canada has, therefore, long been an object of jealousy to these man-dealers, in order to prevent it from existing as a place of security to their pseudo-property. It was from this circumstance they strived to make of Canada a second Texas, knowing well that whilst it owned the British power, Slavery received a check on the North American Continent. (Hear.) Nor is the prejudice against colour, or persecution of the coloured race, confined to the South; it exists, and in a formidable degree, in the North; and were the British sway to cease in North America, if we lost our sovereignty on the St. Lawrence, the United States of America would become one large bazaar of Slaves. I need but refer you to the riots and destruction of property at Boston—the conflagration and destruction of the Pennsylvanian Hall at Philadelphia—the foul murder of Mr Lovejoy at Illinois—and the exclusion of coloured persons from society and the professions, to prove my case. (Cheers.) From these facts, I think you will come to the conclusion, that the unfortunate beings taken on board the Spanish schooner Amistad, and committed to gaol, and the unfortunate beings now immured in a dungeon to give evidence against them, are but too conclusive proofs of the treatment they may look for at the hands of Americans. But, to turn from this topic, on which I could descant for hours, I proceed to the treatment of the Aborigines in the United States, as contrasted with those in her Majesty's dominions in North America. I am not going to speak of the scandalous violation of the flag of truce, with the concomitant murder of the brave and deceived Osceola—and which all the waters of the Mississippi will never wash away or efface from the long catalogue against the United States—but I will tell you boldly, that, whilst our efforts in Upper Canada have been sedulously directed to raise to the highest scale of being the poor benighted savage of distant parts, the American Government is adopting still more vigorous measures to cut off the Indians from all happiness, whether mental or bodily, and repulsing every advance they may make towards that state in the scale of being man is appointed to enjoy. Every compact made with these much oppressed sons of the soil, appears to be an experiment of how far American duplicity and avarice can be carried on the one hand, and Indian credulity and endurance on the other. In short, all treaties entered into between the Executive and the Indians, are, on the part of the latter, a contract by which they engage to lose much and gain but little; and, after ratification, with a fatality attending all engagements between a wolf and a lamb, some obstacle arises to the white man's performance of his treaty. Oh! how emphatically may the poor Indian exclaim, with reference to the Americans, " Timeo danaos et dona ferentes." That such cause of dread, on the part of the red man of the forest, is not groundless, witness that bloody and unhallowed war which has so long been waging against the persevering Seminoles, at such immence sacrifices of life and treasure—a war, by which victory gained by the bayonet and sword, or by the tomahawk and scalping-knife, must weaken the power of the commonwealth—a war, in which aggression and tyranny are contending against moral right and natural justice. (Shame.) The poor persecuted Cherokees, who cast one fond, long, lingering look behind, as they were driven from the homes of their sires to the far West, is another of the flagrant enormities perpetrated against these simple aborigines of the American Continent. Now, contrast the Indians under the British sway ;—view their noble, faithful conduct at Caughlawaga : themselves unarmed, and surprising and capturing a band of armed men arrayed against the British authorities—(cheers)—and the conduct of the Indians and coloured people of Upper Canada also must prove to you how earnestly they entreat of you to resist, by all means in your power, the dismemberment of the empire, and the downfal of that dominion, on the Continent of North America, on which the social happiness, freedom, and prosperity of so interesting a people is completely and inseparably interwoven. They pray of you to maintain the colonial empire of Great Britain, full, entire, and inviolate, on every ground of justice, goodness, patriotism, and humanity. (Much cheering.)

The Rev. Dr. Heugh adverted to the magnitude of the objects which the Aborigines Society had in view, and stated a variety of reasons to show why the vastness of the subject, and the obstacles which lay in the way of success, should not operate in making them shrink from the labour of overpowering them, but rather should incite them to redoubled diligence. He pointed to the fact that in this, as in every other work of Providence, great minds were rising up to bestow their energies in the cause, and that, backed by the influence of public opinion, and the blessing of God upon their endeavours, they could not fail to be successful. He reprobated the idea of individuals keeping back from the struggle, on the ground that their individual labours could be of little or no use in the great contest. They should recollect that the shower was made up of drops, that the river was swelled out by the flow of small streamlets, and that the host was composed of units. They never ought to despair of a good cause. The first thing in allying themselves with any cause was to ascertain its quality. If the cause was a bad one, let them leave it off, and it will come to nothing ; but if it was a good cause, let them prosecute it with confidence, in the divine approval, and with the certainty of victory. After asserting the principle, that error could not always maintain its sway, but that ultimately it must give way before the force of eternal truth, and that, in the cause of humanity and justice, the Christian might ever calculate on the favour of God, the Rev. Doctor pointed out the benefits which their efforts were calculated to confer upon the millions of our fellow-subjects in India— benefits of great temporal value, but still more valuable as affecting their eternal destiny. He observed, that great blame attached to the people of this country on account of the injuries inflicted on the aboriginal inhabitants of our Colonies—it was formerly a sin of ignorance, but now no such plea could be brought forward ; and awful would be the responsibility, if the country did not exert its authority to put an end to the atrocities committed in its name. The honour of Christianity required that they should support the Aborigines Protection Society. He did not know how the honour of Christianity could be hurt more than by associating injustice with it. It was truly said in the case of individuals, that that man did more injury to Christianity than any Infidel could do, who lived in sin under a profession of Christianity ; but if this was the case in regard to individuals, how much more was it the case in regard to nations. If a nation professed Christianity, and, as a nation, practised wickedness, did it not do much to prejudice the Christian name in the eyes of other nations? The Rev. Doctor moved the first Resolution, which was seconded by JOHN REID, Esq., viz. :—

" That this Meeting, having heard the highly important and interesting statement now given by Sir C. E. SMITH, Bart., respecting the Objects of the Aborigines Protection Society, and the details he has now communicated, regarding the condition of the Aboriginal Inhabitants of our Colonies—together with the information so obligingly and voluntarily furnished by Dr. THOMAS ROLPH, from Canada—renews the pledge formerly given, that, approving of the Objects of the Aborigines Protection Society, they will co-operate with, and aid that Society to the utmost of their power."

Dr. WATSON moved a vote of thanks to Sir C. E. SMITH and Dr. ROLPH —which was seconded by Mr SMEAL :—

" That the best thanks of this Meeting are due, and are hereby tendered, to Sir C. E. SMITH and Dr. ROLPH, for the very able, and interesting, and eloquent Addresses they have now delivered, on the Subject of the Aborigines in the British Colonies."

Sir C. E. SMITH, in acknowledging the compliment, concurred in the remarks made by Dr. Heugh, relative to the injury done to Christianity by nations as well as individuals, in acting contrary to the Christian rule. He spoke of the great interests, in relation to the eternal welfare of the Aborigines of our colonies, which their present efforts were subserving, and observed, that in promoting the good, both temporal and eternal of others, we were at the same time promoting our own; for it held as true now, as it did at the time it was written, that " he that watereth will be watered again." The more of spiritual benefit we gave to them, the more we would be benefited ourselves—for, if principle spoke true—if Scripture spoke true—if history spoke true, there never was a nation that did so, but that nation received, in the providence of God, tenfold more benefit to itself.

Dr. ROLPH also acknowledged the honour done him, in a few appropriate remarks.

Mr JOHN MURRAY then read a Memorial to Government on the subject of the Amistad, which was unanimously agreed to :—

" Unto the Right Honourable VISCOUNT MELBOURNE, the Right Honourable VISCOUNT PALMERSTON, and the other Members of her Majesty's Cabinet:

" The MEMORIAL of the GLASGOW EMANCIPATION SOCIETY, and other Inhabitants of Glasgow, in Public Meeting assembled, the 15th October, 1839:

" Showeth,

" That your Memorialists are deeply interested in the Abolition of Slavery and the Slave Trade throughout the world, and in every thing connected with that subject, or with the interests of Africans, wherever or however they may be oppressed.

" That your Memorialists have lately heard through the public prints— especially the *New York Emancipator*—of the singular and peculiarly interesting case of the Amistad, Spanish schooner, bound from Havanna to Port-Principe, in the Island of Cuba, with a cargo of Africans lately imported there as Slaves ; who, to regain their liberty and return to Africa, rose upon the Whites, and after having, as is alleged, killed the Captain, took possession of the vessel, and ordered the remaining Whites to steer for the coast of Africa: but, being betrayed by them, the Amistad was navigated to the coast of America, and, on the 26th August last, was captured off Culloden Point, near New London, by the United States brig Washington, Captain Gedney. The Africans, then amounting to 40, were imprisoned in New Haven on the charge of piracy and murder, and the survivors, except four children who were retained as witnesses, were brought up for trial at the Circuit Court at Hartford, Connecticut, on the 17th ultimo ; while Jose Ruiz and Pedro Montes, who were transporting them as their property from Havanna to Principe, knowing them to have been, only a few days before they sailed, illegally imported, and were thus guilty of felony, were, it appears, allowed to go at large, the Spanish Minister residing in the United States taking no cognisance of their offence.

"The Court, it appears, decided that it had no jurisdiction in the charge against the Negroes ; but it is said, that the Spanish Minister Plenipotentiary, Don Anjel Calderon de la Barca, demanded that they should be given up to the Spanish authorities in Cuba, which there is great reason to fear will be complied with; for it is not likely that, following the very liberal example of Great Britain in regard to American Slaves put ashore on British territory, they will free them and then pay for them.

"Fearing this result, and seeing that they were illegally imported into Cuba, contrary to the Treaty entered into by Spain with Great Britain for the suppression of the Slave Trade, and therefore that they were not Slaves, but freemen—and, as 'malice prepense' could not be imputed to them, they cannot, in the eye of the law, be deemed guilty of murder, but, at the utmost, justifiable homicide, if not rather, under all the circumstances, and by the practice of law, exonerated entirely from all criminality and accountability, as being illegally held in captivity, they were entitled to effect their escape by any means in their power.

"Your Memorialists, therefore, entreat the British Government to interpose its power and influence, by every legitimate means, with the American or Spanish Governments, to have these Africans set at liberty, if possible, in America, where they may be taken care of as they have already been, by the American Anti-Slavery Society ; or, if too late to secure that, that they be liberated at Cuba by the Mixed Commission Court there, and handed over to a British ship of war, to be carried back to Africa, if possible to the port from whence they were taken, and escorted to their homes, and that the whole transaction be properly and distinctly explained to them, so that none of the criminality connected with their case may be imputed to Great Britain, but that they be made to understand that Great Britain is entirely opposed to the Slave Trade, and is desirous that every Tribe in Africa would oppose it also, and would trade in the productions—not the *people* of Africa."

Mr WM. SMEAL proposed a Memorial praying the Government not to recognise the independence of Texas. Before reading the Memorial, Mr S. read the following Resolutions, passed at a meeting of the Glasgow Emancipation Society in March, 1837, which evince that the Society has long kept a watchful eye upon this important question.

"Resolved:—That it appears fully evident to this Society, that the struggle to achieve the independence of Texas is not a struggle for the acquirement or maintenance of civil and religious liberty, but for the privilege of *holding Slaves*, and carrying on the *Slave Trade;* and that the triumph of the Texian arms would, therefore, be calamitous to the cause of universal freedom.

" That the 9th Section of the Constitution, adopted by the revolted Texians, demonstrates the inconsistency and falsehood of their profession of attachment to the principles of righteous liberty—is an infamous and wicked document, reflecting the deepest disgrace upon · its framers, and deserving the unmitigated execration of mankind.

" That the offer made by the Texians to the United States, of an ex-clusive monoply of the Trade in Slaves, should have been resented as a gross insult to the moral sense of the nation ; and that its acceptance is a melancholy proof of the deadening and demoralising influence of the Slave system.

" That we regard, with the highest admiration and respect, the exalted and independent conduct of the Honourable John Quincy Adams, in the United States' Congress, in pleading for the Emancipation of the Slave, and in exposing the very suspicious conduct of the United States' Government, in regard to Mexico and Texas."

The Memorial proposed by Mr Smeal was then read and agreed to, amid cheers :—

> " Unto the Right Honourable VISCOUNT MELBOURNE, the Right Honourable VISCOUNT PALMERSTON, and the other Members of Her Majesty's Cabinet:
>
> " The MEMORIAL of the GLASGOW EMANCIPATION SOCIETY, and other Inhabitants of Glasgow, in Public Meeting Assembled, the 15th October, 1839:

" Showeth,

" That your Memorialists are deeply interested in every measure which may affect the Universal Abolition of Slavery and the Slave Trade, and, being informed that a Minister from Texas, the revolted province of Mexico, has arrived at the British Court, for the purpose of prevailing upon Her Majesty's Government to acknowledge the Independence of that Territory as a separate State or Republic, they feel themselves called upon to enter their protest against a measure fraught with such imminent danger to the cause which the British people have, for many years, struggled to promote, and made so great a sacrifice to obtain.

" Although in their present character principally concerned for the effect the proposed measure may have on the Abolition of Slavery and the Slave Trade, your Memorialists may be permitted to remark, that, as British subjects, they are not indifferent to the political bearings of the question upon British interests—whether Mexico, after setting such a noble exam-ple by freeing her own Slaves in 1829, shall remain an Independent Re-public of Freemen, or be partitioned out piecemeal—as Texas has been permitted to be—into Slave States, and be united in succession to the Southern Slave States of America ; for your Memorialists have no doubt that the recognition of the Independence of Texas by Great Britain, and other European Powers, is only a prelude to its annexation to the United States, and is particularly desired by the Slave-holders, that they may be the better able to overpower the Abolition movements in the Northern States.

" Your Memorialists deem it superfluous to detail to the British Cabinet the various processes of fraud and violence, by which it has but too success-fully been attempted to sever that Province from Mexico, and in which the Revolters have been treacherously aided by the Republic of the United

States of America; while Great Britain looked indifferently on. Had General Gaines' stratagem been acted on the Canadian frontier, the British Government would have felt keenly the treachery, but she permitted Mexico to suffer, when a simple Remonstrance,—as suggested and received with cheers in the House of Commons,—would probably have prevented the separation of Texas.

" Your Memorialists observe that, by the ninth section of its Constitution, Texas is constituted a Slave State—for it declares that all Slaves emigrating to Texas shall remain in that State ; that the Congress of Texas shall pass no laws to prohibit Emigrants from the United States of America from bringing their Slaves into the Republic, and holding them as they were held in the United States. Nor shall Congress have power to Emancipate Slaves—nor shall any Slave-holder have power to Emancipate his or her Slaves, without the consent of Congress, unless sent without the limits of the Republic ; and no free person of African descent, either in whole or in part, shall be permitted to reside permanently in the Republic ; and, it is added, the importation of Africans or Negroes into the Republic, excepting from the United States of America, is prohibited and declared to be piracy.

" Such being its Constitution, the Inhabitants, who now desire the recognition of its Independence, are not native Texians, but Slave-holders, with their Slaves, principally from the United States, and land speculators ; and it thus holds out a ready market for the superabundant Slaves from Virginia, and the Slave-breeding States of America.

" Your Memorialists have had too much experience of the result of Laws made in Slave States, to restrain Slave-holders, to believe that the last clause above cited can, in the least, prevent the importation of Slaves from Africa, and are persuaded that various means will be devised to evade it, and that it is evaded by Slavers touching at the extreme outports of the United States, whence the Slaves are transported to Texas ; and also by false clearances and otherwise. And your Memorialists may be permitted to cite the authority of Mr Buxton, that, ' in the last twelve months, 15,000 Negroes were imported from Africa into Texas ;' and he adds, ' I can conceive no greater calamity to Africa than that Texas should be added to the number of Slave-holding States—it is a gulf which will absorb millions of the human race.'

" Your Memorialists, therefore, entreat that, for these important reasons, and many others which might be adduced, and in consideration of the earnest desire so prominently and permanently evinced by the British People, for the Universal Extinction of Slavery and the Slave Trade, that you will be pleased to refuse to recognise the Independence of Texas, unless the Texians consent to Emancipate all the Slaves at present there, and so to alter the Constitution as to prohibit for ever the holding of Slaves in the Territory of Texas."

Mr LANGLANDS then proposed a vote of thanks to Dr. Wardlaw and the Trustees for the use of the Chapel, and observed, that the Rev. Doctor would have been present but for other engagements. He also moved a vote of thanks to the Chairman.

The CHAIRMAN acknowledged the compliment, and the meeting separated.

BRITISH INDIA SOCIETY.

No. V.

COMMITTEE ROOM, GUILDHALL HOTEL,
September, 1839.

SIR,—The accompanying Papers will explain the circumstances under which the Committee have the honour to address you,—will make known the names of the gentlemen who compose it, and the authority by which they have been constituted.

Encouraged by the confidence placed in them, and supported by the unanimous Resolutions passed on the 6th July, at Freemason's Hall, the Committee desire to state, that their object is to interest you, and all others within the circle of your influence, in promoting the great cause proposed as the end and aim of this Society, namely, " the bettering of the condition of our fellow-subjects, the Natives of British India."

Deeply sensible of the moral strength and importance to the cause, arising from the disinterested advocacy of persons like yourself, the Committee earnestly hope to enrol your name as a member, and will thankfully receive an intimation of your intention to join the Society.

We have the honour to be,
SIR,
Your most obedient Servants,
On behalf of the Committee,   F. C. BROWN,   ⎫
GEORGE THOMPSON, ⎬ *Secs.*

P.S. Since the Meeting above alluded to, intelligence of another famine which is afflicting Western India, has been published. " Famine still continues to desolate the Province of Kattywar. The inhabitants are flying in great numbers, and parents selling their children for a few mea. sures of grain.—*Asiatic Journal, Sept.* 1839, p. 67.

A Donation of Ten Guineas, or an Annual Subscription of One Guinea, constitutes a Member. Donations and Subscriptions will be received by the " LONDON AND WESTMINSTER BANK," at Lothbury; 9, Waterloo Place, Pall Mall; 213, High Holborn; 12, Wellington Street, Borough; 87, High Street, Whitechapel; 155, Oxford Street, and by their corres. pondents throughout the country; or by Mr Thomas Boulton, Collector.

RESOLUTIONS

Unanimously passed at a Numerous and Most Respectable Public Meeting, held at Freemasons' Hall, on Saturday, 6th July, 1839.

THE RIGHT HONOURABLE LORD BROUGHAM, IN THE CHAIR.

I. THAT the present Condition of our Native fellow-subjects, in British India, estimated at a hundred millions,—wholly excluded from the privileges of representation, and under the dominion of a government, in whose appointment they have no voice, and over whose acts they have no control,—demands the active sympathy and constant vigilance of the British People.

II. That it is established by ample evidence, that there exists throughout British India a great amount of poverty, misery, ignorance, and discontent ;—that immense Tracts of Land are suffered to lie waste ;—that the Revenue is declining ;—that the People are oppressed by grievous Monopolies, extending even to the Necessaries of life ; that the ancient public works are perishing ;—that the Internal Communications have been neglected ; and that dreadful Famines frequently devastate the land.

III. That these evils exist in a Country of vast extent and great fertility, whose Inhabitants are docile, intelligent, and industrious ; whose ancient Institutions might be made instrumental to good government—a Country capable of supplying many of our demands for tropical produce, and the desire and capacity of whose population to receive the manufactures, and thus stimulate the Commerce of Great Britain, would, under a just and enlightened rule, be incalculably developed.

IV. That for the purpose of obtaining and diffusing information—of directing more efficiently the public attention to a subject involving no less our commercial and political interests, than our social and moral duties— and of suggesting and giving effect to such measures as are likely to improve the circumstances, and provide for the happiness of the people of British India, an Association be now formed, to be called, " THE BRITISH INDIA SOCIETY, FOR BETTERING THE CONDITION OF OUR FELLOW-SUBJECTS —THE NATIVES OF BRITISH INDIA."

V. That a Committee be appointed, consisting of the following Gentlemen, (with power to add to their number,) who are requested to draw up the necessary rules for the government of the Society, and to direct its proceedings for the year ensuing :—

COMMITTEE OF MANAGEMENT,

With power to add to their number.

WILLIAM ADAM, Esq., late of Calcutta.
WILLIAM ALDAM, jun., Esq., Leeds.
JONATHAN BACKHOUSE, Esq., Darlington.
W. THOMAS BLAIR, Esq., Bath.
HENRY BLANSHARD, Esq.
JOHN BOWRING, Esq., L.L.D.
MAJOR-GENERAL BRIGGS, (Treasurer).
LORD BROUGHAM.
F. C. BROWN, Esq., Tellicherry.

N

Thomas Christy, jun., Esq.
Thomas Clarkson, Esq.
John Crawford, Esq.
Sir Charles Forbes, Bart.
Thomas Frankland, Esq., Liverpool.
John Harford, Esq., Bristol.
William Howitt, Esq.
John Hull, Esq., Uxbridge.
Joseph Pease, Sen., Esq., Darlington.
John Stewart, Esq.
George Thompson, Esq.

REASONS

WHY IT IS THE INTEREST OF EVERY PERSON IN THE UNITED
KINGDOM TO PROMOTE THE OBJECTS OF THIS SOCIETY.

SUGAR.

Annual Loss.

The present annual import of Sugar into the
United Kingdom, was, in 1838, 235,700 tons,
which cost, freight and charges included, in
bond, at £42 a ton, ... £9,899,400
If the Natives of India were allowed to hold their
own land on the same terms as British subjects
elsewhere, the same quantity of sugar could be
there produced, and sold in Great Britain at
£18 a ton, in bond, ... £4,242,600

Consequent annual loss to Great Britain, . . £5,656,800

Note. The import of Slave-grown Sugar into
foreign Europe, in 1838, was 281,000 tons; the whole
of which might be produced in India.

COTTON.

The present annual import of Cotton,
is, . lbs. 411,286,783
Deduct E. Indian, „ 55,577,197

Leaves of Slave-
grown Cotton, 355,709,586 cost, at 7½ per lb. £11,115,925
Cost of the same quantity of East Indian Cotton,
if the Natives were allowed to produce it on
their own land, on the same terms as American,
at 2d. per lb., would be, . . . £2,964,246
Annual loss to Great Britain, ... £8,151,679

Note. The Cotton papers, published by the Court
of Directors in 1836, establish the fact, that freed
from Land Tax, Cotton can be grown in almost
every province throughout India, at 1d. per lb.;
see also evidence which follows.

SILK.

The present annual import of Silk,
   is,   lbs. 6,000,000 cost of which at 15s. per lb. £4,500,000
Deduct East
   Indian,   „ 1,500,000

Leaves of fo-
   reign Silk,   4,500,000
Cost of this quantity of good East Indian Silk, if
   the Natives were allowed to produce it free of
   Land Tax, would be, at 12s. per lb.,   .   £2,700,000

      Annual loss to Great Britain, ...   £1,800,000

RUM.

The present annual import of Rum is 4,993,942 galls.
Of which taken for home consumption 3,324,709 „
The present price of this quantity of Rum in bond,
   at 3s. a gallon, is, ...   £498,706
The same quantity of East Indian Rum could be
   delivered at 1s. 6d. a gallon, .   .   .   249,353

      Annual loss to Great Britain, ...   £249,353

COFFEE.

The present annual import of Coffee is, lbs. 40,000,000
Of which Ceylon and East Indian, is, „   9,000,000

                              31,000,000
Cost of which, at 100s. per cwt., is, .   .   £1,383,925
Cost of the same quantity of East Indian Coffee,
   if the Natives were allowed to grow it, Land
   Tax free, on the same terms as British subjects
   elsewhere, would be, at 44s. per cwt.,   .   608,927

      Annual loss to Great Britain, ...   £774,998

TOBACCO.

The present annual import of Tobacco,
   is, ...   lbs. 50,000,000
Of which is East Indian,   .   „   50,000

Leaves of Slave-grown Tobacco,   „ 49,950,000
Cost of which, at 6d. per lb., in bond, is, .   £1,248,750
Cost of the same quantity of East Indian Tobacco, if the Natives were allowed to produce
   it, Land Tax free, would be, at 1d. per lb, in
   bond, ...   208,125

      Annual loss to Great Britain, ...   £1,040,625

LINSEED.

The present annual import of Linseed,
is, ... bushels, 3,500,000
Of which is East Indian, . , 300,000

Leaves of foreign Linseed, . . 3,200,000
Cost of which, at 40s. per qr. of 8 bushels, in bond, is, £800,000
Cost of the same quantity of East Indian Linseed,
if the Natives were allowed to grow it, Land
Tax free, 3s. for 84 lbs., or 14s. 3d. $\frac{3}{7}$ the qr.,
in bond, ... £285,714
Annual loss to Great Britain, ... £514,286

NOTE. "The annual consumption of Linseed in
Great Britain, on an average of 5 years, is 2,500,000
bushels, of 50 lbs. each, which would be dead weight
of 300 ships: that double this quantity, (yielding 5
per cent. more oil than Russian,) might be supplied
by India, there cannot be a question."—*Bell's View
of the Commerce of Bengal, for* 1834-35.

FLAX.

The annual consumption of foreign Flax for three
years, to 1839, is, . . tons, 69,255
Average value at £50 per ton, is, . . £3,462,750
Flax, (which is the stem of the plant producing
the Linseed,) in India rots on the ground!
If the Natives were suffered and encouraged,
there is no doubt that the same quantity could
be prepared in India, and sold in Great Britain
at £18 per ton: the cost, therefore, of 69,255
tons of Flax would be, . . . £1,246,590
Annual loss to Great Britain, ... £2,216,160
Total annual loss, or excess in price paid by
Great Britain, on the foregoing eight staple
articles alone, exclusive of Rice, Indigo, Hemp,
Oils, Wool, Tea, Drugs, Dye Stuffs, &c., &c.,
all produceable in India, at the same propor-
tionate low prices, exclusive also of the loss to
British Shipping, is, ... £20,403,901

NOTE. The length of the coast line of the British
Isles is 2800 miles. The length of the coast line of
India, from the mouths of the Indus west, to Mergui
east, cannot be less than 7000 miles.

	Ships.	Tons.
The total shipping of India in 1838, was	321	95,301
The total shipping, inwards and outwards, from the one port of Stockton upon Tees, was, in 1838,	8,027	993,578

REVENUES OF INDIA.

The annual revenues of India are stated to be,
Parliamentary Return 1837,—Land Tax, £11,317,017
Opium, Salt, and Tobacco Monopolies, Inland
and Sea Customs, and other Taxes, . £6,741,395
Total, ... £18,058,412

The charges for conducting the Government of India at home and abroad, Interest of Debts, &c., equal the sum total of the revenue. If, therefore, Great Britain defrayed the whole amount of those charges, paid the dividends on East India Stock, and the Interest of about Forty Millions of Debt owing in India, leaving the Native Tax free, to produce in return all that she requires for her commerce and manufactures, the clear gain to the country would amount to several millions a year.

NOTE. Indian Debt in 1837, £39,766,478.—*Mont. Martin*, p. 346.

MANNER IN WHICH IS EXPENDED MORE THAN ONE HALF OF THE ABOVE SUM OF £20,403,901, LEVIED ANNUALLY UPON THE PEOPLE OF GREAT BRITAIN; OR, REASONS WHY IT IS THE DUTY OF EVERY PERSON IN THE UNITED KINGDOM TO SUPPORT THIS SOCIETY.

SUPPORT OF SLAVERY AND THE SLAVE TRADE.

It is now proved that 375,000 Africans are annually sacrificed as follows :—

		Dollars.	
Perish in the passage,	37,500		
Die from seizure, march, detention, &c.,	187,500		
Survive and are sold in the Slave States and Colonies of America, &c.,	150,000 at 150 ds. a head	22,500,000	
At 4s. 6d. to the dollar,			£5,062,500

This fact is attested by two testimonies published by Mr Fowell Buxton: one a letter to himself, dated May, 1838, from Governor Maclean, of Cape Coast, stating that the net profit upon a Slave is from 150 to 200 dollars, when sold in Cuba and the Brazils: the other, the calculation of the Sierra Leone Commissioners, who give for an outlay of 100 dollars, a return of 280.—*Buxton on the Slave Trade*, pp. 89 and 90.

The trade yields, therefore, a profit so euormous, as to make it morally certain, that, so long as this profit can be got, no power on earth will put down the traffic ; nor can any Princes or States, however well intentioned, enforce Slave treaties.

East Indian free labour costs 3d. a day, African Slave labour, 2s. The fund for paying Slave labour, and the fund required for buying Slaves, must, it is evident, be the money paid for Slave-grown products. This fund is mainly derived, *directly and indirectly*, from the excess of price paid by Great Britain to the Slave Cotton-growers of America for their Cotton, amounting,

as shown above, to, ...	£8,151,679	
To the Slave Tobacco-growers for their Tobacco,	1,040,625	
To the Slave Coffee-growers for their Coffee,	774,998	
Add annual cost, in money only, of the Squadron fruitlessly employed on the Slave coasts,* .	650,000	
		£10,617,302

But Cotton in the United States being more profitable than Sugar, the United States resort to Cuba and the Brazils, for one half of the Sugar required for the population. This quantity now amounts to about 50,000 tons annually, costing, at £42 a ton, ... £2,100,000

As the wants of America will keep pace with her doubling population, and as she will never want the means of paying for their supply with the money she is sure of receiving from Great Britain for her Cotton, it results that a constant, regular, and rapidly increasing demand is created for the Slave-grown Sugar of Cuba and the Brazils, and with this demand, a regularly increasing demand for more Slaves, by whose labour alone the Sugar required can there be grown. Hence the vast increase of the Slave Trade, proved to have taken place of late years, and hence the known aggravated condition of the Slave.

PROOFS OF THE FOREGOING STATEMENTS.

TAXATION AND TREATMENT OF THE NATIVES OF INDIA.

LAND TAX. December, 1821.

Orders of the Court of Directors to the Government of Madras, 12th Dec., 1821. Para. 99.

The Court of Directors order the Government of Madras to demand the whole rent of the land as land-tax. " WE are aware that the difficulty lies in ascertaining the degree in which, in all the variety of cases, the surplus produce already is, or is not, absorbed by the Government demand. But this is the difficulty which exists in forming or adjusting the settlement everywhere. Minute accuracy cannot be obtained ; but in making the best approximation to it in our power, we shall avoid all material evil if the surplus produce (i. e., the whole rent of the land,) is, in all cases, made the utmost extent of our demand."

Orders of Sir Thomas Munro, afterwards Governor of Madras, to his Assistants, the Land-Tax Collectors, and Assessors.

1812. Fifth Parliamentary Report, Appendix " The ryots (cultivators) when left to themselves, always pay their rent (land-tax) in preference to every other debt.

---

* Mr M'Queen rates the expence connected with the suppression of the Slave Trade, at between £600,000 or £700,000 per annum to this country, and he calculates, that the total expence since 1808, exceeds £20,000,000, independently of the compensation money of £20,000,000.

xx. pp. 748, 749.
Sir Thomas Munro's orders to his assistants.
—Bad crops are the chief cause of failures.—Whatever may have been the crop, *should it have even been less than the seed sown*, they (the cultivators) should always be made to pay the full rent if they can.—Whether or not a ryot, who asks a remission, can pay his rent, may, in most cases, be discovered, by ordering the amount of his failure to be assessed upon the village.—In the same manner, when a village fails, the balance upon it is (to be) assessed upon the neighbouring villages.—The amount of this second assessment ought seldom or ever to exceed 10 per cent. of the rent of the ryots of the inferior village, on which it is imposed. If a balance still remains, it should be assessed upon all the villages which constitute the mouza (the hundred,) but not in a greater proportion than 10 per cent. of the rent. Should a part of the balance yet remain unextinguished, it ought to be remitted."

Ibidem, p. 786, para. 12. Sir Thomas Munro to the Board of Revenue.
" The increase of these articles (Indigo and Sugar) is occasioned by an extra land-rent, *amounting to twice or three times the ordinary rate*, to which all land employed in their cultivation was subjected, and this increase is likely to go on progressively, as the demand for them is great."

20th June, 1838.

Bombay Government Gazette, 20th June, 1838.

The permission to cultivate land with fine cotton and the Mauritius sugar cane in Bombay, annulled by the Court of Directors.
" The Honourable the Court of Directors having been pleased to disapprove of the Notifications of the 24th of February and 1st August, 1835, and of the 1st and 17th November, 1836, issued under the authority of Government by the Revenue Commissioner, granting certain exemptions from assessment (land-tax) to land cultivated with cotton and the Mauritius sugar-cane, and to direct that such notifications be immediately recalled; the Right Hon. the Governor is pleased hereby to cancel the said notifications from this date."

18th Jan., 1839.

Bombay Government Gazette, 18th January, 1839.

" It is hereby notified for general information, that in conformity with section 18, of Act 1, of 1838, the Hon. the Governor in Council is pleased to exempt the following articles, the produce of the Bombay Presidency, from (sea) customs, viz. :—

Onions, pot-herbs, and garden stuff, eggs, poultry, and fish, exempted from sea customs in Bombay for the first time, in 1839.
1. Onions, Potatoes, Greens, Pot-herbs, Garden stuff generally, and Fresh Fruits in the ordinary acceptation of the terms. 2. Eggs and Poultry. 3. Fish, fresh and salted, with the exception of Shark's Fins and Fish-maws."

1830.

Testimony of a Committee of the House of Commons, 1830.

House of Commons Report.
" The whole system (of land-tax) resolved itself, on the part of the public officers, into habitual extortion and injustice ; whilst what was left to the ryot (cultivator) was little more than what he was able to secure by evasion and concealment."

Rev. Howard Malcom. 1837.

Testimony of an American Eye-witness, the Rev. Howard Malcom, of Boston, U. S.

Beauty of the country from Cuddalore to Tanjore.
Taxes and other causes keep down the labourer to a
" Feb. 1837. A more beautiful country than that from Cuddalore to Tanjore (Madras) cannot possibly be imagined. The dense population and rich soil give their energies to each other, and produce a scene of surpassing

state below the southern slaves of America. loveliness ; *but the taxes, and other causes, keep down the labourers* TO A STATE BELOW THAT OF OUR SOUTHERN SLAVES.

Government share of the rice crops about 50 per cent., but the collection amounts to three-fourths of the crop. Other taxes are monopolies, duties on exports and imports, licenses, fees " The Government share of rice crops is, on an average, about 50 per cent.! But the mode of collection (in money) causes the cultivator to pay about three-fourths of his crop. The public treasury is further replenished by monopolies, by duties on exports and imports, for the most part heavy ; by licenses for the sale of arrack and toddy ; by stamps ; by fees on judicial proceedings, &c., &c." on judicial proceedings, stamps, &c.

Moisture alone necessary to constant cropping in India. " As there is always power enough in a tropical sun to produce vegetation, moisture alone is necessary to constant cropping. Districts, therefore, furnished as this is with tanks and rivers, present continually all the varieties of seasons in Europe. The eye wanders over large fields, in some parts of which men are ploughing, in others planting, and in others harvesting, at the same time. Most of the lands are cropped twice a-year, sometimes with rice, but more frequently with rice first, and then some other grain or pulse. *The scene is beautiful; but squalid poverty and miserable mendicants constantly intrude,* and remind one of Pope's lines—

Every variety of season produced by irrigation. Employment of the ryots, and mode of cropping.

But squalid poverty every where intrudes.

" In vain kind seasons swell the teeming grain,
Soft showers distil, and suns grow warm in vain ;
The swain, with tears, his frustrate labour yields,
And famished dies, amidst his ripened fields !"

India asserted to be in a state of progressive poverty and depression. Hamilton, author of the Gazetteer, his testimony to the fact and causes. " All the writers I have been able to consult, and most of my friends in various parts of Hindostan, declare India to be in a state of progressive poverty and depression. The following observation of Hamilton embodies the general idea. After stating many facts, and adducing public records to prove his assertion, he says :—" All the offices of emolument, civil and military, and the highest lines of commerce, are in the hands of strangers; who, after a temporary residence, depart with the capital they have accumulated. Under native rulers, even the extortions of rapacity, and the drains of tribute, returned into circulation, and promoted in some degree territorial industry. Under its present constitution, the remittance, or rather tribute to Britain, carries off every year a large share of the produce, for which nothing is returned."—*Travels in South Eastern Asia, including Hindostan,* Vol. ii., pp. 69 to 90.

Bishop Heber. *Testimony of Bishop Heber, an Eye-witness.*

The land-tax occasions the poverty of the natives. " The natives of India are just as desirous of accumulating wealth, as skilful in the means of acquiring it, and as prone to all its enjoyments, as any people on earth. It is the LAND-TAX THAT CONFIRMS THEIR UNALTERABLE POVERTY."

Mr Rickards. *Testimony of Mr Rickards, a Company's Servant in Bombay.*

The Government seizes every where upon half the pro- " From the impure fountain of the (Mahomedan) financial system, did we, to our shame, claim the inheritance of duce of the land as tax, upon the pretence that the Mahomedans so did. a right to seize upon half the gross produce of the land as a tax; and wherever our arms have since triumphed, we have invariably proclaimed the savage right."

Hon. F. J. Shore. 1836.

Testimony of the Hon. F. J. Shore, a Company's Servant in Bengal.

The Government not by right, but by might, assesses the land-tax at pleasure, and in default of payment, offers the land at public auction.
The Government fixes the assessment on the new occupier at its own valuation.
Districts compared to an apple in a cider press, each succeeding collector feeling his prospects and reputation depend upon the amount of revenue he extracts.

" The Government possesses, not by any right or justice, but by the assumption of might, the power to assess the revenue (land-tax) at pleasure; to demand what it pleases from the owners, farmers, cultivators, or whatever they may be denominated ; and in default of payment, it offers the land at public auction, to realize the sum demanded, at the same time fixing the assessment on the new occupier at its own valuation, and treating him in the same manner, if he fails to pay it.

" Every district has been like an apple in a cider-press, while the collector turns the screw ; and when he has squeezed it to the extent of *his* power, makes over the handle to another, and he to a third, and so on. *A collector, is, in various ways, made to feel that his reputation and prospects depend upon his realizing a large revenue, and that a recommendation for a reduction in the amount of the assessment, is only considered in the light of a register of his own inefficiency.*"

Mr W. Adam. 1838.

Testimony of Mr W. Adam, an Eye-witness, and official Reporter upon Education in Bengal, in 1838.

Fear inspired by the appearance of Europeans in native villages : the language of kindness unintelligible to the people.

" The sudden appearance of a European (Englishman) in a village often inspired terror, which it was always difficult, and sometimes impossible, to subdue. The adoption of such a style of address by a Government functionary (as consulting their wishes and feelings) was apparently new to them, and scarcely intelligible."

1832. Francis Warden, Esq., an East India Director.

COTTON.—*Testimony of Francis Warden, Esq., an East India Director. Appendix to Report of Select Committee,* 1832.

States the Government land-tax in Guzerat on the Cotton there grown is 1¼d. per lb.

" It requires fourteen beegas of land (about seven acres) to produce a kandy of 864 lbs. of (Guzerat) Cotton, on which the Government assessment (land-tax) therefore is, rupees 56, or, at 1s. 9d. the rupee, 4l. 17s., averaging 1¼d. per lb.—In the Surat division it averages 1.55d. per lb., in Kaira 1.13d., in Ahmedabad 1.53d., in the S. Mahratta country 1.14d. In Kattywar the assessment exceeds 5l. a kandy."

16th Dec. 1838.

Testimony of an Eye-witness, an English Cotton Merchant, addressed to the President of the Chamber of Commerce, Manchester.

MANCHESTER, 16th Dec., 1838.

Guzerat Cotton taxed 50 per cent.

SIR,—During my stay in Guzerat, in the spring of 1837, I was occupied several months in purchasing, cleaning, packing, and shipping East India Cotton.—The Cotton grown in Guzerat (the best in India) is taxed by the Honourable Company at a rate which often

106

Often injured before cleaning. proves 50 per cent. of its market value. The Cotton, with the seed in it, (called kupass) as it is taken from the plant, is often very much injured before cleaning. It is in this state that the Honourable East India Company levy their land-tax on it. Immediately after it is gathered, it is brought (by the tax-gatherers) into the Government kullies (yards); and if the growers, or owners, are not immediately prepared to pay the tax upon it, the kupass is buried in the ground, as a farmer would his winter potatoes in England, except that there is no straw or matting placed between the earth and the Cotton. The top is covered with large lumps of earth. I presume this method has been resorted to on the part of the Hon. East India Company to avoid the slight expense of building sheds, and has been connived at on the part of the dealers and cultivators, because the moisture to which it is thus exposed strikes through the Cotton, and very much tends to increase its weight, and improve its appearance for the time being; but when it is packed in a moist state, mildew naturally follows, and before the Cotton reaches England, the colour is very much deteriorated.

Land-tax levied in the seeded state.

Every pound is brought by the tax-gatherers into the Government yards; if the cultivator is not then able to pay the tax, the Cotton is all buried in holes dr'g in the gr'nd, and lumps of earth piled upon it.

Hence the moisture strikes thro', and when packed, the Cotton becomes mildewed.

Difficulty in taking out seed, in consequence of the earth thus mixed with it, and impossibility of separating the earth. The kupass (unseeded Cotton) also becomes mixed with lumps of hard earth, and, as it cannot be passed through the seeding machine without being beaten out, to facilitate the fibres leaving the seed, to which they are very tenacious, these lumps of dirt are broken up into a fine brown powder, which cannot afterwards be extricated from the Cotton.

Omrawuttee Cotton is grown at the rate of 2 lbs. for twopence; Government takes one half for land-tax, hence the remaining one pound costs the grower twopence. I am informed that the Omrawuttee Cotton is grown at the rate of two pounds for twopence, in moderately favourable seasons, but as Government, who neither sow nor reap, take one-half of this as their land-tax, the remaining *one* pound stands in twopence to the grower.

The Patells, or heads of villages, to whom Government look for the payment of all demands, oppress the poor ryots (cultivators,) in the same ratio as Government is arbitrary in its exactions upon the Patells.

Irrigation beneficial to Cotton. I am convinced, in my own mind, that the effect of judicious irrigation would be exceedingly beneficial. For five months, until the plant comes to maturity, it has no rain. The nature of the plant, consequently, does not fully develop itself.

Indispensable to the finer varieties. In support of my idea regarding irrigation, I would call your attention to the fact, that no good Cotton from warm climates is imported to Great Britain, that has not been irrigated, as Egyptian Cotton, for instance; and in Peru, Cotton could not be grown at all without artificial irrigation. Even in India, many articles are irrigated, such as Sugar, Tobacco, and Chilies.

All lands in India that are irrigated, whether naturally or artificially, pay double land-tax; consequent effect upon the prices of raw produce. But I am informed, on undoubted authority, that all irrigated lands in India are doubly taxed, (sometimes trebly and quadruply;) so that, supposing that with the expences of irrigation, three pounds of Cotton could be grown for fourpence halfpenny, the Honourable East India Company would take, under such circumstances, two pounds as their share; and consequently, the remaining one pound would cost the cultivator fourpence halfpenny.

Testimony of the Bombay Chamber of Commerce.

Bombay Chamber f Commerce,1837.

To the Chief Secretary to Government.

BOMBAY, *4th March,* 1837.

Delay in fixing the amount of land-tax on Cotton. SIR,—I am requested by the Chamber of Commerce most respectfully to bring to the notice of the Right Honourable the Governor in Council, the situation in which the Cotton-dealers in the Broach Collectorate are now placed, owing to the annual Assessment (land-tax) on the Cotton for the Revenue not having been yet fixed.

Prevents the shipment of the Cotton to Bombay, also the cleaning, seeding, and preparing. Until this assessment has been made, *the Cotton cannot be shipped* for Bombay, nor, unless under certain restrictions, not available to all the dealers, *can the Cotton be cleaned and prepared for shipment.*

The nature of the climate, making the time very short for these processes. Under the most favourable circumstances, the time for effecting all this is, from the nature of the climate, necessarily very short.

Which any delay curtails, and is felt as a great hardship. Any delay in fixing the Assessment, still further curtails the very short period the climate allows, and is felt as a very great hardship.

Testimony of the Right Honourable Holt Makenzie, a Company's Servant in Bengal.

Rt. Hon. Holt Makenzie. 1838.

India capable of producing the best Cotton, witness its past produce. " India would not be found wanting in any essential requisite for the production of the best Cotton. The vast extent to which Cotton has long been grown, and the exquisite beauty of some of its manufactures, are only additional reasons for prosecuting inquiry."

Testimony of Dr. Spry, a Company's Servant in Bengal.

Dr. Spry. 1838.

India sealed against the enterprize of Britons in order to prolong the abuses of patronage. " It is certainly without a parallel in the annals of the world, that a country possessing such capabilities as India, should have been so long hermetically sealed against the enterprise of Britons, in order to prolong the abuses of patronage.

Had the peninsula been open, England would not now depend on America for Cotton. Had the peninsula been open, we should not now be dependant upon America for raw Cotton, nor would the country have been brought, as it was four years ago, to the very verge of bankruptcy and revolution, when the stock of Cotton was not adequate to three week's consumption.

Slavery in the United States the consequence. To this astounding blunder the Southern division of the United States owes its Cotton plantations, and its rice fields, and also the blighting curse of Slavery.

That Cotton equal to American can be grown in India proved by evidence. Evidence confirms the fact, that Cotton can be grown in India, fully equal, or rather superior, to the bulk of American." *(Modern India.)*

Testimony of American Cotton Merchants.

1839. (Extract from a New York Circular.)

American Cotton Circular; danger apprehended " It is however advisable not to draw the cord too tight by these financial arrangements, (alluding to the plans in to American Cotton if the cord be drawn too tight. discussion for holding the coming crop of Cotton,) lest by the attention of Great Britain being turned to the cultivation of Cotton in India, *from which, doubtless, exhaustless supplies can be obtained,* we may be in danger of losing that market."

The New York Evening Post, Aug. 1839. *The New York Evening Post, Aug., 1839, quoted in the Money Article of the Times of Sept. 6th.*

American explanation of the rise in the price of Cotton. " The cupidity of John Bull has been excited by our State Stocks bearing, as they do, a greater interest than his Consols, and for the last three years he has poured out his substance in loans to us, by which means we have artificially raised the price of Cotton.

Its effects, as manifested in the present state of England. " At length a disastrous season forces poor John to pay out the solid stuff to the sturdy farmers of Germany, for bread to eat ; and as he had no remittances for account of our importers from the continent of Europe, or elsewhere, as of old, to countervail this new drain, he was soon in the state of a man who has loaned out his money on such security, that he cannot avail himself of it, when most needed, and, at the same time, has a large and expensive family to maintain and provide for, without any receipts from the sale of his merchandise, which has suddenly fallen on his hands to a merely nominal value.

The probability of another commercial crisis, as in 1825, anticipated. " The continental markets reject honest John's manufactures ; we drain his ready money ; and between the two, he is likely to enlarge a second edition of the purging of 1825, much to his improvement, and eventual restoration to health."

W. Felkin, Esq. 1839. SILK.—*Testimony of W. Felkin, Esq., F.R.S.*

The following paper was read at the British Association at Birmingham, in August, 1839. Extract:—

Capacity of India to produce Silk in any quantity required by Great Britain. " But the chief object in view in bestowing the time and labour, necessary to bring about the results which establish the interesting and important fact, that SILK of the best quality could thus be grown here, (in England,) was to show how the produce of this article, so well adapted to the soil and climate of that country, (India,) and the condition of its multitudinous inhabitants, (and so necessary as raw material to one of our chief manufactures,) might be greatly improved in quality, and indefinitely increased in quantity, in Hindostan. There, labour is cheaper than anywhere besides, and land, unoccupied and waste, but perfectly suitable for the Mulberry, is plentiful ; so that, by introducing into Hindostan the superior kinds of silk-worms, and Mulberry trees, so long grown in the south of Europe, and recently brought forward with such vast enthusiasm in the United States of North America ; the whole might be supplied from India with raw Silk at half its present cost, a cost increased by the demand greatly exceeding the supply, so as to have compelled us to pay four, instead of three millions sterling a year, during the last four years, for the same weight of material, and thus greatly to limit the extent, and even to risk the safety of the Silk manufacture itself."

TEA. TEA.—*The present annual Import of Tea is* 40,000,000 *lbs., costing, upon an average, at* 1s. *per lb., in Bond,* £2,000,000 *sterling.*

This Tea has hitherto been chiefly paid for, by smuggling into China, a poison there prohibited by the Government on pain of death—that is to say, Opium.* This Opium, the natives of India are compelled to produce, it is then all taken from them, under severe penalties, at a price fixed by the Government, and retailed by the Government at a monopoly price to purchasers, who smuggle it into China. The past consequences of this monopoly have been, that the British consumer has paid at least one-fourth more for his Tea than its natural price, and that British manufactures have been thereby excluded from China. The present consequences are, that the Chinese Government has confiscated three millions sterling of Opium, (British India property;) and hence has annihilated capital to that amount; it further stopped the trade, and made prisoners of all the European residents at Canton, as Opium smugglers.

* "The Chinese Emperors have suppressed it, (Opium) in their dominions, by condemning to the flames every vessel that imports this species of poison, and every house that receives it."—*Raynal's Indies*, b. iii., p. 413, ed. 1777.

The future consequences to Great Britain will be, to be drained annually (in the absence of the cheap staples of manufacture to exchange with the Chinese,) of about two millions in bullion, being the prime cost of the Tea required for the population.

To India the consequences will be, to be further taxed to the extent of a million and a half a year, in order to make good the loss produced by the monopoly Opium being unsaleable. It is now known that 100 chests of Tea, produced in India, are on their way to England, leaving not a rational doubt, that if the natives had been encouraged to produce Tea, Land Tax free, forty years ago, Great Britain would be now receiving her supply from her Indian dominions, guiltless of the enormous losses sustained by British merchants, guiltless of the enormous evils entailed upon India by the monopoly, and upon China by the traffic in that drug.

OPIUM MONOPOLY.

Thelwall's Iniquities of the Opium Trade. 1839.

Testimony of an Eye-witness in Bengal.

The culture of the Poppy forced upon the Natives. Surveillance of the police over them, and consequent sufferings.

" The evils of the cultivation (of Opium) do not end here. In consequence of being obliged forcibly to cultivate this highly taxed drug, the peasant is constantly exposed to a suspicion of retaining some part of the produce for private sale ; the surveillance of the police is, therefore, especially directed to these unhappy creatures ; and the oppressions which they are subjected to in this way surpass belief. They are exposed to every sort of annoyance which the ingenuity of these authorized plunderers (the police, and the custom-house searchers) can devise, in order to extort bribes. The privacy of their miserable abodes is intruded upon by these harpies of Government, and no redress can be given by the Government unless they abolish the production of this accursed drug. When the Government itself is virtually the defendant, an appeal to its justice is a mockery.

Bribes extorted from them.

Hopelessness of appeal to Government.

Vast tracts of land now covered with Poppies, which are not cultivated on waste or barren lands; the reason why.

"Vast tracts of land, formerly occupied with other articles, are now covered with Poppies, which require a superior soil to produce Opium in perfection. Hence its cultivation has not extended over waste and barren lands, but into those districts and villages best fitted for agricultural purposes, where other plants, grown from time immemorial, have been driven out before it."

Famines.
Famine of 1838.

The inevitable consequences resulting, are, periodical famines. Last year, (1838,) one of these visitations destroyed 500,000 persons, (or about three times the entire population of Liverpool,) in North Bengal; while, at the same time, nearly 156 millions of pounds weight of rice only were being exported to foreign parts from South Bengal. The English Magistrate of Agra, the capital of North Bengal, states, in his official return, (*Bombay Times*, June, 1839,) that 144

144 children carried off by wolves, as stated by the magistrate.

children had been carried off by wolves; so completely had the famine annihilated every thing eatable in the country, but the children that were left to the survivors.

RESULTS TO GREAT BRITAIN.

Results to Great Britain.
* M'Culloch's Dictionary, p. 443.

Three millions of persons now depend for subsistence upon receiving the Cotton of America.* Upon the security of this Cotton and of other crops, many millions of British capital are freely lent, serving to raise and keep up the prices of produce. This rise prohibits British manufacturers from executing their orders, and stops their mills. Idleness and hunger in the starving operatives, who are the immediate victims, breed disaffection to the Government, and hatred to all established institutions. The retail tradesman, who lives by their industry, suffers and feels with them. Men see the vast and complicated evils, and under the delusion that has been propagated relative to India, confess the impossibility of applying any legislative remedy. Foreign nations believe the heart of the country to be diseased. Foreign navies are created and forced into existence. High profits abroad enable a high interest to be paid for capital, borrowed in order to establish manufactories designed to rival, and one day certain to supplant those of England.

RESULTS TO THE WORLD.

Results to the world.

Africa is made day by day, and year by year, a more gigantic, appalling scene of man-stealing, war, and human butchery: America is cursed with unmitigated and unmitigable Slavery: India is beggared and re-barbarized: China is defied and demoralized; and Europe, Asia, and America, are all being sown with the seeds of wars and contentions, in which England's best heart's blood will be poured out.

This Exposition is submitted, for dispassionate inquiry and examination, to every lover of his country and friend of his kind.

Committee of the British India Society. London, Sept., 1839.

NOTE.—As the *Glasgow Emancipation Society* is pledged to sustain the British India cause, contributions to the Funds of the Glasgow Society, *will effect the same object* as if remitted to London.

PERSECUTION IN JAMAICA.

No. VI.

THE attention of the Friends of Religion, Justice, and Freedom, is earnestly solicited to certain iniquitous proceedings which have recently taken
place in Jamaica, which, if not promptly and vigorously met, threaten, not
only the ruin of those against whom they have been directed, but the destruction of that liberty which has been purchased for the Negro at so
costly a sacrifice.

At the Assizes for the County of Cornwall, held at Montego Bay, in
July last, various actions were brought, under different pretexts, against
several well known friends of the labouring classes in that Island. Amongst
the victims of these proceedings, were a clergyman of the Church of England, a Missionary belonging to the Baptist Society, and some of the
Magistrates specially appointed for the protection of the emancipated population, in each of which cases the Jurors have decided against the party
accused, and in most of them with enormous damages, under circumstances
which can leave no doubt that the design is to ruin those whose hatred of .
oppression had rendered them obnoxious to the enemies of freedom.

At the same Assizes, a criminal information, filed by order of the Court
against the Editor of a local Newspaper, for grossly defaming a Baptist
Minister, was tried, and the Jury, without the formality of retiring to consider their verdict, immediately acquitted the defendant, contrary to the
express direction of the Chief Justice, and the plaintiff was left with his
injuries unredressed, and a heavy amount of legal expenses to pay.

These violent and reckless proceedings appear to have produced a greater
excitement than has been known in the Island since the insurrection in
1832.

The Negroes behave with admirable moderation, but they feel most
deeply at the prospect of their best friends and protectors, of whom it was
once sought to deprive them by brute force, now falling victims to the
more specious, but not less effectual weapons of oppression, in the form of
legal proceedings.

The Juries, on these occasions, were almost wholly composed of persons
belonging to a class who have uniformly and bitterly opposed the Abolition
of Slavery, and the friends of the Anti-Slavery cause, and there is no hope
whatever of obtaining justice for the parties against whom these verdicts
have been given, but by an appeal to the Court of Error in the Island, and,
if requisite, to the ultimate tribunal in this country, which will involve
heavy legal expenses, in addition to those already incurred.

To meet these expenses, an earnest appeal is now made to the liberality
of the British public.

COMMITTEE.

The following Gentlemen have been appointed a Committee, with power to add to their number, to lay the particulars of these atrocious proceed-ings fully before the public, to promote Subscriptions for the purposes contemplated, and similar cases of oppression, and to superintend the ap-propriation of the funds collected:—

LONDON.

SAMUEL GURNEY, Esq., Treasurer.

Charles Lushington, Esq., M.P.
T. F. Buxton, Esq.
William Allen, Esq.
Rev. John Dyer.
George Stacey, Esq.
G. W. Alexander, Esq.
Rev. I. J. Freeman.

Robert Forster, Esq.
W. B. Gurney, Esq.
Joseph Cooper, Esq.
John Scoble, Esq.
Jacob Post, Esq.
Rev. J. Woodwark.

HENRY STERRY, Secretary.

PROVINCIAL.

Thomas Clarkson, Esq., Playford Hall, near Ipswich.
Joseph Sturge, Esq., Birmingham.
J. T. Price, Esq. Neath.
James Whitehorn, Esq., Bristol.
Rev. Thomas Scales, Leeds.
William Chapman, Esq., Newcastle-upon-Tyne.
Isaac Bass, Brighton.
J. B. Pease, Esq., Darlington.
R. D. Alexander, Esq., Ipswich.
W. D. Crewdson, Esq., Kendal.
W. T. Blair, Esq., Bath.

William Wilson, Esq. Nottingham.
John Cropper, Esq., Liverpool.
Rev. John Birt, Manchester.
G. H. Head, Esq., Carlisle.
Joseph Eaton, Esq., Bristol.
Richard Rathbone, Esq., Liverpool.
Joseph Marriage, jun., Chelmsford.
Henry Sparkes, Esq., Exeter.
Jona. Backhouse, Esq., Darlington.
C. Hindley, Esq., M.P.
Anthony Wigham, Esq., Aberdeen.
Thomas Pewtress, Esq., City.
William Smeal, Glasgow.

The following Subscriptions have been already received:—

Samuel Gurney, Esq.,		£100	0 0
Mrs Darby and Family, Coalbrook Dale,		100	0 0
Joseph Sturge, Esq., Birmingham,		50	0 0
G. W. Alexander, Esq.,		50	0 0
James Cropper, Esq., Liverpool,		50	0 0
John Cropper, Esq., do.		50	0 0
W. B. Gurney, Esq.,		50	0 0
G. H. Head, Esq., Carlisle,		50	0 0
J. T. Price, Esq., Neath,		50	0 0
Edward Smith, Esq., Sheffield,		50	0 0
Mrs A. H. Smith, Olney,		50	0 0
John Bell, Esq., Wandsworth,		25	0 0
W. G. Gibson, Esq., Saffron Walden,		25	0 0

Jonathan Backhouse, Esq., Darlington, . .	£20	0 0
Joseph Eaton, Esq., Bristol, ...	20	0 0
Miss Margaret Pope, Staines, . . .	20	0 0
Thomas Clarkson, Esq., Playford Hall, . .	10	0 0
Richard D. Alexander, Esq., Ipswich, . .	10	0 0
Edward Pease, Esq., Darlington, . . .	10	0 0
John Sturge, Esq., Birmingham, . . .	10	0 0
Charles Sturge, Esq., do., . . .	10	0 0
Francis Gibson, Esq., Saffron Walden, . .	10	0 0
Mary Gibson, do.,	10	0 0
Ann Gibson, do.,	10	0 0
John Backhouse, Esq., Darlington, . . .	5	0 0
William Backhouse, Esq., do. . . .	5	0 0
Joseph Cooper, Esq., ...	5	0 0
Charles Lushington, Esq., M.P., . . .	5	0 0
Joseph Pease, Esq., M.P., ...	5	0 0
J. B. Pease, Esq., Darlington, . . .	5	0 0
George Stacey, Esq., ...	5	0 0
Henry Sterry, ...	5	0 0
John Penny, Esq., ...	3	0 0
Ann Backhouse, Darlington, . . .	2	0 0
A Friend, per Joseph Sturge, . . .	2	0 0
Captain C. R. Moorsom, R.N., . . .	2	0 0
A Friend, per Rev. J. Woodwark, . . .	1	0 0
T. Pewtress, Esq., ...	5	0 0
Robert Grahame, Esq., of Whitehill, Glasgow, now residing		
at Weymouth, ...	10	0 0
William Allen, Esq., Plough Court, . . .	5	0 0
D. Anderson, Esq., ...	5	0 0
N. W. Bromley, Esq., ...	1	0 0
Charles Burls, Jun., Esq., 19, Bridge Street,	0	10 6
Baptist Church, South Silver Street, Aberdeen, .	4	11 0
John Thomas Bigg, Esq., ...	10	0 0
J. J. Cobbin, Esq., Stock Exchange,	2	2 0
Mrs Davies, Walthamstow, ...	2	0 0
Rev. John Dyer, ...	1	1 0
Robert Forster, Esq., Tottenham, . . .	3	0 0
Friends at Buckingham, per Rev. J. H. Hinton, .	2	10 0
W. F. Lloyd, Esq., 56, Paternoster Row, . .	1	1 0
Joseph Neatby, Esq., Kennington, . . .	5	0 0
Richard Peek, Esq., Haselwood, Devon, . .	10	0 0
Miss Phillips, Wandsworth, . . .	10	0 0
Price of Sugar, 112, Strand, . . .	5	0 0
Do. & Co., Mincing Lane,	5	0 0
Jacob Post, Esq., Islington, ...	2	0 0
William Peckover, Esq., ...	10	0 0
E. Prentis & Co., ...	10	0 0
Willian Risden, Esq., Burlingham House, Pershore, Wor_		
cestershire, ...	21	0 0
Rachel Stacey, Tottenham, ...	3	0 0
Rev. James Smith, Astwood, . . .	5	0 0
Joseph Sharples, Esq., ...	20	0 0
John Tawell, Esq., Southwark Bridge Road,	2	2 0
Sarah Wedgwood, per Joseph Sturge, Esq.,	10	0 0
Josiah Wedgwood, Esq., London, . . .	20	0 0

	£	s	d
John Wilkinson, Esq., Wycomb,	£5	0	0
W. Wailes, Esq., Leeds,	5	0	0
Thomas Wontner, Esq.,	2	0	0
Benjamin Young, Esq., Hatfield, Herts,	5	0	0
Thomas Brewin, Esq., Birmingham,	2	0	0
John Childs, Esq., Bungay,	1	0	0
Rev. J. A. James, Birmingham,	1	0	0
G. Newman, Esq., Leominster,	5	0	0
John Pritchard, Esq., do.,	5	0	0
Nathaniel Roberts, Esq., per Rev. J. Woodwark,	10	10	0
Samuel Southall, Esq., Leominster,	5	0	0
T. & W. Southall, Birmingham,	2	0	0
J. Bird, Esq., Oakhampton,	0	10	0
C. Bowley, Esq.,	5	0	0
J. Buller, Esq.,	10	0	0
W. Flanders, Esq., Woburn Place,	2	0	0
R. Holborn, Esq.,	1	0	0
Richard Porter, Esq., Deptford,	1	0	0
G. Pearse, Esq., Stamford Court,	1	0	0
W. Pearse, Esq., do.,	0	5	0
J. Pearse, Esq., Oakhampton,	0	5	0
Rev. G. Richards, Stamford Court,	0	10	0
C. J. Tosswell, Esq., Torrington Square,	2	0	0
Edmund Waller, Esq., Lowton,	5	5	0

Subscriptions will be received at the following places:—

Samuel Gurney, Esq., Treasurer, Lombard Street; Messrs. Herries, Farquhar and Co., Bankers, St. James's Street; Messrs. Drewett and Fowler, Bankers, Princes Street, City; Messrs. Hanburys, Taylor and Lloyd, Bankers, Lombard Street; Baptist Missionary Society's Office, Fen Court, Fenchurch Street; J. H. Tredgold, Esq., Secretary to the British and Foreign Anti-Slavery Society, 27, New Broad Street; or by any of the Members of the Committee.

Subscriptions will be received in Glasgow, by WILLIAM SMEAL, 161, Gallowgate.

GLASGOW:
Printed by AIRD & RUSSELL, Buchanan Court,
75, Argyll Street.

CPSIA information can be obtained
at www.ICGtesting.com
Printed in the USA
BVHW051121181218
535875BV00020B/817/P

9 780259 957454